1980

YOUR
FORTUNE
IN
FRANCHISES

YOUR FORTUNE IN FRANCHISES

RICHARD P. FINN

 Contemporary Books, Inc.
Chicago

Library of Congress Cataloging in Publication Data

Finn, Richard.
  Franchising.

  Includes index.
  1. Franchises (Retail trade)—United States.
I. Title.
HF5429.3.F54   1979   658.8′4   78-27585
ISBN 0-8092-7449-3
ISBN 0-8092-7448-5 pbk.

Published by Contemporary Books, Inc.
180 North Michigan Avenue, Chicago, Illinois 60601
Manufactured in the United States of America
Library of Congress Catalog Card Number: 78-27585
International Standard Book Number: 0-8092-7449-3 (cloth)
                                    0-8092-7448-5 (paper)

Published simultaneously in Canada by
Beaverbooks
953 Dillingham Road
Pickering, Ontario L1W 1Z7
Canada

Contents

1

What Is a Franchise?

Many individuals spend all of their adult lives wishing fervently to run their own businesses. Perhaps you too see this as an avenue leading to that elusive life of ease for your family. You will have the independence that being your own boss brings. You will have security because no one can fire you. Your income will be higher because you can collect a salary along with a profit or return on your invested capital. You will have the pride of ownership that is so rare, occurring only with a home, a boat, or an expensive automobile.

Regrettably, the cards have become increasingly stacked against the small businessman's making it big operating alone. There are just too many headaches, too many diversions from the task at hand, and too much competition.

Fortunately, there is still one way where success is assured, where most of the key decisions such as how to price your goods or service are made for you and yet you can put your own stamp of individuality, in a sense, on the business. I am

1

talking about franchising—a very old method of merchandising that has garnered its greatest success since World War II. Today, there are over 1,200 firms offering franchises and over 700,000 small businessmen holding franchises in businesses that are grossing well over $280 billion in sales per year. One-third of all retail sales today are franchise sales. It is fair to state that franchising is one of the fastest growing industries in the history of this nation. The industry must be doing something right.

Studies by the U.S. Small Business Administration, U.S. Chamber of Commerce, and Dow Jones Service Company indicate that 80 percent of all new independent businesses fail in the first year, and 92 percent of them fail in the first five years. Meanwhile, only 20 percent of all new franchises fail in the first year, and only 3 percent fail during the first five years of business. Stated another way, if you go into business for yourself, chances are eight in ten that you will fail in the first year and better than nine in ten that you will fail during the first five years. As a franchise, your chances are eight in ten that you will succeed in the first year and well over nine in ten that you will survive the first five years of business.

Franchises are now available in an unbelievable range of businesses. Such fast-food franchises as McDonald's, Wendy's, Kentucky Fried Chicken, Pizza Hut, and Carvel Ice Cream get most of the publicity. However, there are literally hundreds of other fields represented, and the number of areas grows yearly. Since the energy crisis, franchises covering fireplace equipment and solar heating have emerged. Other new areas, including tax preparation, security systems, quick copying, real estate brokerage, water treatment, lawn care, equipment rental, pet shops and guard dogs, campgrounds, and swimming pools are catching on rapidly.

Individual franchisees come from virtually every walk of life. Some have been successful even though they possessed little or no previous business experience. Others have technical or professional training that could be utilized in their new business. Others were formerly cooks, salesmen, mechanics, office workers, sales clerks, executives, engineers, or industrial workers. They were all attracted, as you should be, by the proven success of the "franchise package" that appeared clearly superior to what they could produce on their own starting a small business from scratch with a little capital and a lot of hope.

The package that today's franchisor offers is so comprehensive that no individual could hope to equal it, in my opinion. It embraces, for the most part, the following elements: an established business name and reputation; nationally advertised brands or services; modern, eye-appealing store design; carefully chosen store locations; standardized procedures and operations; and comprehensive training, financing, and research. Such a package promises a substantially reduced risk of failure along with good to excellent income.

For a franchise to work properly, there must be advantages for both parties involved—the franchisor and you, the franchisee. If this were not the case, both parties would stand a much greater risk of failing. In franchising, you derive one huge intangible advantage of starting out in a business that has already been successful for many others. You are protected by the umbrella of a recognized, presold brand name and established reputation. You use not only the franchisor's product but also his know-how in every operating area.

By combining your resources with the franchisor in a continuing relationship in which both parties share the profits and expenses, you can start your business with much less capital than would be required to start and run a complete, independent, unfranchised outlet. A large part of the total marketing and start-up cost is divided among the franchisor and thousands of individual franchisees. Such costs include promotion, advertising, centralized buying, market research, facility and equipment plans, site evaluation, accounting systems, and so forth. Everyone involved works for the benefit of all. No individual businessman, working for himself alone, could accomplish this.

There is no fixed pattern for dividing initial financing

burdens among franchisors or franchise systems. Some franchisors choose to extend credit to franchisees for equipment, inventory, or supplies by selling to you through installment contract or security agreements, by direct leasing or subleasing of equipment and/or your premises, or by guarantees of credit extended by others. Many franchisors will not extend credit to you directly but will help you obtain credit locally. Or the franchisor may assume any secondary or contingent liabilities.

By the same token, some franchisors find that leasing and subleasing your quarters, or the lease and sale of equipment used in the business, represents a source of profit. They may also find that this represents the most effective means of ensuring proper locations or quarters for you. This is because the markets for borrowing money, real estate, and construction are very competitive at all times.

You should receive initial start-up and continuing services from a franchisor. Which services you obtain, or how much service is granted, depend upon the type of franchise involved. The most frequently provided services include:

1. Market surveys and aid in selecting a suitable site where location is an important business factor. For example, a fast-food franchise would demand a high traffic, main thoroughfare location, whereas a home-cleaning service might be located anywhere.

2. Negotiating leases or providing lease evaluation standards and plans, and specifications for facility design, construction and layout.

3. Training and operating manuals, accounting systems, and record-keeping materials.

4. Aid in procuring financing for the above and for the initial franchise fee.

5. Start-up assistance at your location with you and any employees in the first weeks of operation, plus planned preopening promotional assistance.

After your franchise business gets off the ground, the

franchisor will continue to provide valuable assistance. This should include:

1. Periodic employee retraining or training for new supervisory personnel in the event of turnover.

2. Periodic inspection to verify and assist in assuring maintenance of product or service quality and standardizations in accordance with designated characteristics and specifications.

3. Promotion, advertising, and merchandising materials and a regional and/or national as well as local advertising program.

4. Merchandise selection assistance and inventory control aids, marketing data aids, or voluntary centralized purchasing.

5. Assistance in buying and financing equipment.

6. Auditing, bookkeeping, and record-keeping services.

Of course, the above assistance is subject to some variance, depending largely on what type of franchise is involved. It is wrong to assume that all franchises are alike. In fact, there are three rather distinct types. They are:

1. Those that are primarily concerned with an effective method of distributing the franchisor's products. These are found in the auto industry (franchised car and truck dealers), in gasoline stations (any major brand), in bicycles, and in electrical appliances.

2. Those that establish retail outlets where the franchisor is principally selling a name and method of doing business. This type is found in the various fast-food chains, in motel operation, laundry and dry cleaning shops, and various service organizations.

3. Those that establish manufacturing or processing plants such as in the soft drink field, in the baking industry, or in mattress manufacturing.

Product franchising essentially involves a product distributorship franchise where an independent dealer retains his own individual business identity while marketing, along with other products, a trademarked product manufactured by the franchisor, who owns the trademark. In this form of franchising, you usually operate at the retail level. For example, you might run Frank's Bicycle Center and be a franchised distributor for a certain brand of bicycles. As such, you would merely market the trademarked bicycles produced or manufactured by the franchisor. This route, however, has not been the primary thrust of franchising in recent years.

It is much more likely that you will become involved with an "enterprise" franchise. Such franchises depend on harder sell, using clearly identifiable logos and advertising, such as McDonald's or Carvel. In enterprise franchises, the franchisor has a strong interest in making sure that you, the franchisee, conduct your business under his valuable trade name, providing the public with uniform high-quality products and services.

The enterprise franchisor has a legitimate interest in regulating how you sell his products. He will also strive to regulate your sale of products made by others, since they may become associated erroneously with his trade name by the consuming public. Herein lies a very sticky problem. There have been long court battles over how much control the enterprise franchisor should be allowed over the franchisee's products and services. Why the dispute? The franchisor holds that he must prevent the public from being misled as to the nature and quality of the products and services offered under his trademark or trade name. In sum, you get more direct help from the enterprise type of franchisor, but you may also find him more restrictive.

The manufacturing franchise usually operates at the wholesale level instead of the retail level. These include soft drink franchises, which involve a bottling operation, mattress manufacturing, or bakery franchises that sell to retail outlets who in turn sell to the general public. In this type of operation, the franchisor is primarily interested in the manner in which you advertise and merchandise his trademarked products. He is also rightfully interested in maintaining a general reputation to protect the trade name wherever it is used. In sum, the franchisor is mostly concerned with protecting the quality and uniformity of the product rather than in how you run your business.

You can see that the term *franchising* covers a very broad area—perhaps too broad. Some businessmen use the term *franchising* when what they are really offering is a simple distributorship arrangement. In the latter case, the manufacturer sells a product to you at wholesale and you turn around and sell it at retail at a marked-up price. The relationship ends there. There is nothing wrong with such a business relationship; however, it is a far cry from the comprehensive, all-encompassing type of franchise business association that concerns us here.

Part of your problem in understanding the type of relationship lies in terminology. The franchisor is sometimes referred to as the manufacturer, parent company, seller, or licensor—and the franchisee is sometimes identified as a dealer, outlet, associate, licensee, or member. This may seem confusing, but there should be no doubt at all in your mind if the franchisor or manufacturer promises you overnight success today. No legitimate franchisor will promise a get-rich-quick system. While inflated promises were somewhat of a problem in the early days of the industry, in more recent years, increasing government and state regulation, through Uniform Disclosure legislation, has largely ended such questionable practices. This will be discussed in more detail later on in this book.

There are some disadvantages of a franchise arrangement that you should also consider carefully. Not everyone is a potential franchisee. Once you sign a contract, you will give up some measure of freedom. There will be controls placed on you along with constant pressure from the home office to conform to established or newly standardized methods. You will be constrained in making decisions. You may not be able to lower prices directly to meet competition. You may never be able to say that you are really your own boss. If you see these factors as serious obstacles, then you probably should read no farther in this text.

Another potential disadvantage concerns the monetary aspect. You may have to pay a substantial initial franchise fee amounting to many thousands of dollars just for the privilege of sharing the franchisor's secrets. Then, there will be weekly or monthly royalty payments to be made based on the level of your sales. There may be somewhat binding supply contracts with the franchisor for merchandise, supplies, and equipment. How do you feel about this?

Also, you may have to handle a full line of products that includes some items that do not sell particularly well in your locality. You may get the impression that you are doing this so that others in the chain will primarily benefit. While you should receive an exclusive territory for your franchise, these areas may overlap or otherwise provide inequities in your operation. The entire chain may suffer if another area franchisee does not put the same amount of effort into his operation as you do.

The franchise contract itself may contain some provisions that may prove troublesome. Such clauses may impose mandatory working hours well in excess of forty hours or impose unrealistically high sales quotas. The franchisor may also restrict your right to transfer your franchise except by selling it back to the parent company. He may also threaten cancellation or termination of your franchise for some relatively minor infringement.

On the whole, though, it is this author's considered opinion, formed from close observation of the industry for a number of years, that the prospective franchisee today has a stronger position than ever. The government is more than ever intervening on the side of the small businessman franchisee. An organization promoting the interests of all franchisees has been formed out of the coalition of a group of Midwest franchised McDonald's operators. Its voice will likely be heard increasingly. On the other side of the fence, the International

Franchise Association, Washington, D.C., numbers nearly all the reputable franchisors in its growing membership. It is a powerful, effective organization. In the concluding chapters of this book, descriptions will be provided of numerous legitimate, successful franchise operations. It is no accident that all are members of IFA.

In sum, the franchise industry has undergone many changes over the last thirty years or so, and almost all of them are constructive. The risk of your failing in a franchise has lessened greatly. You will have the advantage of the past experience of many others via the trials and tribulations of earlier years. You have the tremendous advantage of emulating a proven business formula. Your franchisor can lead you along the path to success by combining the best aspects of big and small business. That's what a franchise is.

2

Steps to Take before Signing a Contract

Now that you know what the franchise system is all about, and have decided that the system is worth investigating further, you must find a way or ways to become exposed to individual franchise opportunities. One of the great things about franchising is that until the moment that you sign on the dotted line, you can still turn and walk away, having suffered no loss except for a certain amount of time.

However, before you actively seek franchise offers, you should learn all you can about franchises, both from the standpoint of the franchisor and the franchisee. The more knowledge that you have about the various aspects of franchising, the more success you should have in singling out the one best opportunity for you. If you do not take advantage of this learning process, it will be your own fault.

There is plenty of material to study, provided you are willing to take the time. A representative list of leading publications and sources of franchise information is below.

The Small Business Administration
Washington, D.C. 20416

Council of Better Business Bureaus, Inc.
1150 Seventeenth Street
Washington, D.C. 20036

Bureau of Consumer Affairs
Federal Trade Commission
Sixth Street and Pennsylvania Ave. NW
Washington, D.C. 20580

International Franchise Association
Suite 600-W
7315 Wisconsin Ave.
Washington, D.C. 20014

Office of Minority Business Enterprises
Washington, D.C. 20230

U.S. Department of Commerce
Washington, D.C. 20402

The latter organization publishes, and periodically updates, the *Franchise Opportunities Handbook,* a voluminous work that is available at nominal cost from the Superintendent of Documents, U.S. Government Printing Office, Washington, D.C. 20402. This work, the best of its type, lists hundreds of franchisors by group and contains much other worthwhile background information.

In the previous list, IFA publishes a "best seller" called *Investigate before You Invest,* which is an excellent primer on the dos and don'ts of franchising, written in easily understandable language by the organization's legal counsel. The cost is $2.00 per copy. Also, this writer contributes a regular column on franchise subjects to *Income Opportunities,* a leading monthly publication sold on newsstands everywhere. *Income Opportunities* is published by Davis Publications, 380 Lexington Avenue, New York, N.Y. 10017.

You may not be aware that your own daily newspaper is a good source of leads. The classified section of most metropolitan newspapers carries franchise opportunities under the "Business Opportunities" section. Nationally distributed publications carrying franchise ads and information include the *New York Times* and *Wall Street Journal* in addition to the aforementioned *Income Opportunities.*

Some publications reserve certain times for franchise advertisements. For instance, the *Wall Street Journal* generally groups franchise ads together in its Friday editions. Sunday newspaper classified ad sections are excellent places to look. Tear these pages out and keep them in a file folder for handy reference. Or cut out those specific franchise ads that intrigue you and save them.

Another excellent source of information on franchises would be any of the various yearly regional franchise or business opportunity shows. These exhibits, usually sponsored by some local private agency, gather together hundreds of franchisors who are seeking franchisees in that particular area. From your standpoint, it is invaluable to have so many franchisors grouped together under one roof. Visit as many exhibits as you can, and be sure to talk with the representative there. This may give you a feel for the quality of management of the company. Pay particular attention to how these representatives react to your questions. Be very suspicious if vague answers are given. It is highly unlikely that you would ask anything that has not been asked of franchisors previously.

Reputable franchisors typically employ two other general procedures to solicit your interest. First, they may simply advertise the franchise in various media and await a reaction from prospects. Second, they may actively solicit inquiries in markets into which they wish to expand by conducting meetings solely for their own benefit. These meetings may be by invitation only or advertised as open to anyone who wishes to attend.

If you reply to a newspaper or magazine advertisement, the franchisor's first contact with you would be through a letter of inquiry. If it is then determined that you are a serious prospect, he will send you detailed descriptive literature. This would likely be followed up with a telephone call. Some franchisors prefer to call you before they send any written material. The purpose of the first call is to make an initial assessment of whether you are a qualified prospect and whether a later meeting would be appropriate. A detailed qualification questionnaire should be sent to you shortly thereafter.

You should not attempt to read into these early solicitations anything that is not there in black and white. They are intended solely to develop a mutuality of interest. In other words, they show only (1) that the franchisor is legitimate, and (2) that you are a qualified candidate who may become interested in becoming a franchisee. That is all—the bread-and-butter meetings are still to come.

Periodic open public meetings on franchising in general may also prove helpful to you. These meetings involve general discussions of franchising—how a franchise works and what is entailed. Do not expect such meetings to get into the nitty gritty of a particular franchise opportunity. That comes later.

The open meeting does have the advantage of possibly putting you in touch with smaller, regional franchisors. This type of franchise typically is extremely anxious to penetrate new markets because of lack of familiarity of its name. Regional franchisors usually have difficulty in advertising as effectively as large national types. But any franchisor, faced with lagging response to advertising, may adopt the open meeting technique. You have nothing to lose but time in attending one or more of such meetings, which are always advertised in local papers. You can either walk out, free as a bird, or seek further information. You can always talk to the speaker after the program and leave your name and address for future contact.

After these various initial and preliminary contacts comes a really important sequence in the chains of events—the critical first personal meeting. At this meeting, the franchisor is under obligation to provide you with the all-important Disclosure Statement. This statement provides you with all the pertinent background material on the franchise along with the background of the key franchise officials. You must receive a Disclosure Statement at least seven days before payment of any consideration or the signing of a franchise agreement.

The first personal meeting should be invaluable to you. However, you should keep in mind that it is a two-edged sword. Just as you may reject a prospective franchisor as a result of information that becomes evident in the first personal meeting or Disclosure Statement, likewise the franchisor may determine that you do not meet his criteria. The franchisor, in a very real sense, is investing in you by granting you one of his outlets. He may be turning over to you not only his physical facilities but also the goodwill he has built up in the area. He is going to trust you to gain profits and prestige for his company. You may be his ambassador to the consuming public. This is no small risk on his part.

Another thing the franchisor will have in mind in that first personal meeting is that his relationship with you may last for many years. Most franchises run for ten years with a renewal clause. Thus, the franchisor must evaluate you as to character, health, stability, willingness to work, and financial standing.

The franchisor believes that you should be willing to devote long hours to your business. Wealthy applicants are sometimes rejected unless they can show that they can afford to pay someone else to manage their franchise. Absentee landlords are not the key to success in the industry by any means. Your own elbow grease will be an important element.

Make sure that your lawyer attends the first personal meeting. No reputable franchisor will object to this. The presence of a legal adviser attests to your seriousness. Let your lawyer break into the conversation at any time. This will be to your benefit.

One thing that may surprise you in the first personal meeting is that your formal education is not all that important. Many successful franchisees have had only an elementary school education. Business experience is much more important, particularly if there are high technical standards involved in the franchise. I think it is fair to state that reputable franchisors, for the most part, seek successful sales experience and ability, management experience, a favorable community reputation, good credit rating, and capability of meeting investment requirements. Education is way down the list.

The first personal meeting, and later personal contacts with the franchisor, is clearly in your best interest. You should view with suspicion any franchisor who says he will accept you without requiring any personal contact. In fact, a really diligent franchisor may request that your spouse be present at the first personal meeting or at an early subsequent one. Your spouse will likely play an important role in the franchise business and should be made aware of the problems that can arise in operating a franchise.

Subsequent contacts with the franchisor should involve personal interviews with at least one other holder of the same franchise. Since your primary interest is to make money, you want to hear how well others have done and find out, to the extent possible, how reliable the franchisor's income projections have been. Without this information, you would be a rare bird if you had a clear idea of how much money you can realistically expect to make.

The franchisor may include a pro forma profit and loss statement in material presented to you. This is often confusing to many prospective franchisees. The difficulty lies in the fact that this statement may not be representative of the average or median performance of all franchisees in the system. Since you cannot really trust such estimates wholly, you must rely, to a large extent, on what you can learn from field visits.

It is a good idea to obtain a list of current franchisees and then arrange to visit several in your region. Visit these franchisees by yourself without any company representatives present. Engage these franchisees in frank and candid discussion of the product or service and about relations with the franchisor, operating policies, and so forth. Assure these franchisees that your discussion will be kept confidential. It would be well to prepare a list of questions to ask before your visit. Again, be suspicious if the franchisees give vague or evasive answers. For the most part, though, you should find that franchisees will level with you.

If you have reached this stage and you feel satisfied that you should go ahead with the franchise deal, you are probably making the right move. The last step prior to signing a contract usually involves a visit to parent company headquarters, either at your expense or at the franchisor's. Sometimes, the company will reimburse you for travel expenses after you sign a contract.

The visit to company headquarters is very important and should not be avoided. In fact, it is a must. It affords you an opportunity to see how things are run at the top, what kind of middle management the company employs, and how training is conducted. Nine times out of ten your impressions gained during the headquarters visit will be lasting and reliable. They are to your advantage. Each step—each personal contact—is there to reduce the possibility of your investing in a fly-by-night scheme that may result in heartaches and loss of earned money. Franchising, through bitter trial and error over the years, has provided these safeguards for all participants. You would be foolish not to use all of them to the fullest degree.

3

Franchise Fees and Other Financial Aspects of Your Franchise

If you are looking at a franchise deal, there is nothing that you should study more closely than the franchise fee. The fee, and how you pay it, tells you a lot about the franchisor. What it is and how you must pay it will tell you if the deal is too expensive for you. The size of the fee may be important. If the franchise has achieved widespread recognition, such as McDonald's or Midas, you can expect that the fee will be very large. On the other hand, if there is no fee at all, chances are the deal is a distributorship or sales representative-type arrangement and not a traditional franchise at all.

What you are paying for in a franchised business is the permission to use the name and methods of a tried and tested business organization. If every franchisor charged the same fee or used the same method of arriving at the fee, everything would be simple. Instead, you will find wide diversity with regard to fees. We believe that the franchise fee is justifiable because it represents a substantial part of the franchisor's profits. It is charged because the franchisor is "lending" you his years of accumulated know-how and his public image. These factors may be of inestimable value.

You should take nothing for granted in franchise fees, however. A substantial number of gullible individuals have been taken in by unscrupulous operators whose sole interest was the sale of fraudulent franchises. They collected their fees, and the franchisee received nothing in the way of actual assistance. Franchise fees should be for services rendered, and these services should be clearly delineated in writing in a legally binding contract. That is why this observer has long urged serious prospective franchisees to retain competent legal counsel to decipher the jabberwocky contained in most contracts.

In general, you are required to pay a franchise fee in one of the following forms: (a) percentage of gross income, (b) a substantial fixed fee, or (c) a minimal fixed fee. You need to know exactly what you are paying for and what you can expect for your money. You will have to determine how much the prospective franchise business is worth. What will you receive for the price you have to pay?

The difficulty with franchise fees is that they involve both tangibles and intangibles. There is the actual merchandise and material that you receive from the parent franchisor. You can measure in dollars and cents such items as resalable inventory, equipment, store fixtures, and so forth. However, intangibles are not so cut-and-dried and, consequently, it is in the latter area that exorbitant charges are sometimes levied.

A typical franchise fee would be $15,000: payable $5,000 down at the franchise signing, say, in January; $5,000 by June 30 of the same year; and the remaining $5,000 by the year-end. The contract term might be ten or twenty years. A continuing royalty fee of 5 percent of gross sales might be due. A continuing advertising fee of 1 percent of gross sales would also be due.

Most franchisors will provide you with a list of tangible

things that you will receive. You should try to determine the realistic value of equipment provided, such as use of the franchisor's name in image and program, training, site and location approval, operating and merchandising manuals, administrative expenses, periodic visits by field supervisors, grand opening and continuing advertising, initial inventory and office supplies, uniforms, and so forth, and secretarial or other special services. In most cases, you will more than get your money's worth in these items.

It can be said with considerable justification, we think, that the higher the franchise fee, the higher the portion of intangibles included. A franchise company that charges a $50,000 or $100,000 initial fee would very probably be charging an unreasonable fee merely to cover the cost of initial services provided. Moreover, as successful franchises expire and come up for renewal, the franchise fee could then be based totally on the intangible rights of being a member of the system.

In defense of the franchisor, if you can put yourself in his shoes for a moment, intangibles pose problems for him as well. How should he account for the true value of certain items? How much is his name, image, or program worth? How valuable is his training program, which involves keeping you for two weeks at the home office? How much does his advertising contribute to your net income? There are no easy answers to these questions for either party.

You must know what you are getting for the fee or for royalties. The fee may cover training, tuition, and perhaps room and board while you are at the home office training center. The franchisor may even pay you a salary during training, and this may come out of the fee. Equally important for you is to find out if the fee is a single charge, a continuing fee in the form of a sales surcharge, or a fixed fee to be paid periodically. Measure the fee in cost per year rather than as a one-time expense. This should lessen confusion on your part.

Just because the franchise fee is flexible does not mean that there is dishonest intent on the part of the franchisor. The flexibility may be designed to meet a particular situation. A franchise in an area of high potential or excellent traffic location should probably cost more than one located in an area of lower potential. Moreover, it would stand to reason that the first acceptees of a new franchise might pay a lower fee than those coming along years later after the system has gained a strong foothold. Success breeds success.

Some franchisors give you the choice of paying a lump sum at signing or making payments over a specified period of time. Others may require a down payment and either finance the balance themselves or guarantee a bank loan with the franchisee's inventory as security. For your purchase of merchandise from the franchisor, liberal credit terms may be offered or no credit at all may be extended. From the standpoint of the franchisor, the fee accomplishes a lot for him. It creates a stronger bond between himself and you. It may be a continuing source of income for him.

Financing is absolutely vital to the success of any franchise in which you may be interested. I am not just referring to the down payment or initial franchise fee that may get you started. Such capital is really only the tip of the iceberg. You will need a lot more money than that.

You must think in terms of total capital requirements and not just the initial outlays. You have to provide working capital to pull you through the early "rough" months of business. Your franchisor is most likely an understanding businessman. He may be able to keep you out of the soup— but you cannot count on this. Franchise failures almost always occur in the first or second years of operation.

You must plan for adequate working capital for the first several years of activity. Then, if your costs run a little higher or your revenues a little lower than projected, you can offset and adjust accordingly. You may be a little disappointed, but you won't see your life savings go down the drain.

To protect yourself adequately, you should have no confusion in your mind over how much money you need to run your franchise. You should realize that capital represents purchasing power. It includes both funds invested by you and funds made available by creditors. Also, you must be able to differentiate between equity capital and working capital. Equity capital is money invested in machinery, buildings, land, and fixtures. Working capital is money invested in supplies, materials, rent, and wages.

The better you understand all the terms used by franchisors, the better off you will be in dealing with problems later on. It is not too difficult to be misled by terminology, particularly if you are studying sales literature or franchise manual listings. There are important financing terms like *cash required, down payment, equity investment,* and *initial investment* that may mean different things in different franchises.

Further, you should understand that sometimes *initial license fee* includes training and start-up aids and promotions. Sometimes they do not. So your contract must be very explicit. If not, you should hold up until competent legal counsel studies it before giving you the OK to proceed.

You will need the services of an attorney. There are a number of ways that a lawyer can assist you. These include filing the necessary legal papers with federal, state, county, and city agencies and reviewing building and zoning codes, contracts for purchasing an existing business, or aspects of your franchise agreement. If you form a corporation, an attorney can prepare the necessary legal documents required for selling shares in the business. Or he can draw a partnership agreement, if needed. At the other end of the spectrum, if you decide to sell your business, you will definitely require the services of an attorney at that time.

You must not confuse the down payment with ultimate franchise cost. They are not the same. Is there a continuing yearly fee involved? If so, what is it? What is your payment on equipment and inventory? What are the deferred balances, if any? Who finances the deferred balances and at what rate of interest? If the franchisor does not provide this financing, will he help you find someone reputable who does? What commitments for financing can you yourself obtain?

In this regard, you have got to keep a weather eye out for hidden costs. It will come as a shock to you if you find that valuable centralized accounting or bookkeeping services are offered by the franchisor and then learn only later that this service is not free of charge. You must not overlook the cost of finding, buying or leasing, and improving and equipping a business location, obtaining zoning licenses for the operation at that location, and the financing costs involved.

The biggest mistake that you can make, of course, is underestimating the cost of operation. But even before the Grand Opening, many potential franchisees underestimate the cost of initial capital required. This is why many franchisors turn down a substantial number of applicants for financial deficiencies. If you have little or no capital to begin with, it could be a blessing in disguise if you are rejected as an applicant.

Perhaps the real key to success in franchising—from beginning to end—is to line up competent legal assistance. Before you sign anything, you want your lawyer's approval step-by-step. If you do this religiously, there is almost no chance that you will be relying on vague promises of financial support or upon your own hopes and dreams. All the franchise manuals, and the invaluable material put out for the benefit of many by the International Franchise Association of Washington D.C., stress this factor.

Frankly, without competent legal aid, we think the average prospective franchisee is likely to be bewildered by terminology alone. Look in the sales literature under "Financial Assistance Available," and you will find such comments as "Parent company will participate in financing to qualified applicants." Just what does this mean? There is absolutely nothing specific for you to go on. Participate up to what level—10 percent or 15 percent? Or the literature may say, "Financing as needed for qualified applicants." Or "Parent company assists franchisee in arranging needed financial assistance." What do these very broad statements mean? You would be foolish to go ahead on the basis of such vague statements without first obtaining approval from legal counsel.

All financing details in a franchise should be spelled out in clearly understood, nonambiguous language. In fact, we venture to say that the clearer the financing aspects are spelled out, the better the franchise. The really successful and established franchisor—large or small—does not have to try to hoodwink anyone. He wants no misunderstanding. If there is no financing available, you can bet that he will say so clearly. Some very large franchisors have their own small business investment companies from whom you can borrow equity capital. Look for this aspect in preliminary material.

Where exactly will your capital come from? Suppose your cash reserve is insufficient to get started with a franchisor? Borrowing the rest will depend upon a number of factors— what part of the initial cost you will provide personally, your credit rating, your business experience, and the magnitude of your franchise plans. What you put up in equity capital is very important. Your franchisor looks to your equity capital as evidence of good faith on your part. He knows that you must have more than enthusiasm to make it big.

You may find it very helpful to make an inventory of your personal assets, including savings, if the initial financing is a problem. Often, ambitious but capital-short franchisees can take second mortgages on their homes. Or you may be able to use stocks, bonds, savings deposits, or insurance policies as collateral. Perhaps you have friends or relatives who are well-heeled enough to loan you some "seed money." A lot of money has been raised in the latter manner over the years. This can lead to large profits for both you and your backers.

If you are unable to raise money through the above avenues, you can try either commercial banks or the Small Business Administration. As for the SBA, their loans can take the form of actual loans or the participation in, or guarantee of, loans made by financial institutions. SBA assistance is given only to those who cannot obtain it on reasonable terms from other sources. SBA loans can run to several hundred thousand with the usual maximum maturity of six years for working capital and up to ten years for fixtures and equipment. Under some circumstances, portions of a loan involving construction can qualify for terms of up to twenty years. The United States Department of Commerce publishes a list of addresses and telephone numbers of all SBA field offices in the United States. And whether you borrow or not, free financial and management counseling is available at any SBA field office.

Bank lending officers use a very successful technique in dealing with franchisees or small businessmen who must raise capital on their own. First, they want to know how much money you seek to borrow. They know that if you do not know how much money you need and are unable to support your request by a written business plan, you may ask for too little. This could leave you with insufficient capital. On the other hand, you may ask for too much money—there is hardly a better way to have your loan application rejected.

The lending officer also must know the purpose of the loan. It has to make good business sense in order to be accepted. Banks have been burned in a goodly manner by shaky franchise loans over the years. Legitimate loan objectives include purchasing additional inventory, financing accounts receivable, taking discounts on purchase from suppliers, or purchasing some type of new equipment or machinery. What the loan officer will ask himself here is this: "Will this loan contribute to increasing profits in the business?"

Early on, you can expect the loan officer to ask you to identify your primary source of repayment. For instance, short-term operational loans can be repaid from the conversion of assets (usually inventories) to cash. Or the loan could be repaid from profits. A term loan could be paid from additional anticipated profits generated by newly purchased assets. A term loan, for more than one year, requires constant scrutiny by the lending officer. You will have to get used to having him on your franchise premises often. That is part of his job.

The bank lending officer will also insist upon a secondary source of repayment. This is in case your business somehow fails to generate funds through its operation. A secondary source of repayment may be the "general guarantee," or personal guarantee of the owner. After all, your personal resources may be larger than the actual net worth of a brand new franchise business. A personal guaranty may provide rock bottom support for your loan. Other secondary sources of repayment can be collateral owned by your business, such as accounts receivable, inventory, equipment, contracts receivable, or real estate. Personal collateral owned by you that may be acceptable to the bank includes life insurance with cash surrender value; savings accounts; municipal, government, or corporate bonds; time certificates of deposit; marketable securities; or real estate. Also, sometimes a second mortgage on your business residence can be used as collateral.

There are two other possibilities that you can investigate— hypothecation of collateral and subordination of officers' notes. If you own a savings passbook, you may hypothecate this to another person. This person then has power of attorney over the passbook and can legally assign it to the bank as collateral to support the loan. The bank then takes the assigned assets from the businessman as collateral for a loan. When this loan is repaid, the bank returns the collateral to the businessman, who, in turn, returns the passbook to you.

In the second case, a small businessman may borrow money personally for his business, or personally have cash on hand, and lend these funds to the business. Partners in partnerships may also lend their company money and, in return, the business issues a promissory note to the lender. Then, in dealing with the bank, the holders of these promissory notes will subordinate them to all bank indebtedness. This means that in the case of bankruptcy, the bank will be paid before the holders of notes from the business. Obviously, this reduces the bank's risk substantially.

Beyond this, the bank lending officer is going to probe for other backing in your franchise business. Regardless of how small your business seems, it is likely that you will require some accounting help, preferably a certified public accountant. A CPA can better prepare and organize financial statements than you can yourself. Additionally, he may be able to spot opportunities for you to make valuable adjustments. You know the old saying about not being able to see the forest for the trees? This applies here in such areas as collection procedures, tax advantages, and so forth. Also, the CPA knows well the type of information the bank needs to provide it with a clear picture of your operation.

The bank lending officer may appear to be nosey about your affairs, but it is only because he has to be that way. He must know how much you know about the business you are starting. He will probe for weaknesses in your understanding of personnel, advertising, marketing, purchasing, or administration. He will investigate your background fully in terms of education, experience, or specialized training.

The extent of your personal debt is another grey area that will be combed over. This could affect the conduct of your operation, as it may be a large drain when you are required to make withdrawals to pay personal debt. You will likely have to justify your salary to the bank. You will have to show a business plan and a projected income and expense schedule. From this, the loan officer will be able to deduce if you can handle debt service, including loan repayment. Many bankers say that a small businessman should not receive a set salary but should instead make periodic withdrawals for expenses. Of course, it may be possible at the outset that your business will not be able to afford even these withdrawals.

Remember that banks can get pretty testy about how much dough you are putting into a small business. If you are putting up, say, 20 percent and you are asking the bank to put up a much higher percentage, then the bank is really your senior partner in the business. Then the bank is going to be watching closely for losses since they will virtually have to be paid out of the business. If net worth is insufficient, the repayment of your bank loan may be in doubt. This is why bankers expect you to advance what is called equity money as an incentive for you to operate the business in a normal, profitable manner.

You should remember also that bank loan officers do not come from the cookie cutter mold. Two lending officers may evaluate a loan differently. A lot of things will go to make up his decision, but in the final analysis it will be his intuition that will decide. Another factor, of course, will be the general business and interest rate picture. You could be refused cold on one application and welcomed with open arms a few months later, depending upon conditions. On balance though, it will serve you well if you understand lending procedures and are aware of what the lending officer will be seeking before you make an application.

You may be surprised to learn that some negotiation is possible in franchise fees. You can drive a hard bargain if you have extensive business experience or knowledge or have a good potential location. Many franchisors make the amount of investment flexible to meet such personal and economic situations. Franchisees may not be charged the same fee even if they are located in the same geographical area. Franchise deals signed at different times may not have an identical fee. As we said, location may determine size of the fee. Under those circumstances, your chances of driving a bargain may improve, depending upon special considerations. Don't be afraid to dicker with the franchisor. Most franchisors want to and will deal fairly with you.

4

Your Franchisor's Rights

There are no two ways about the fact that your franchisor has the right to impose contractual obligations on you. He must have this right in order to ensure proper quality control—which is mostly what distinguishes his product or service from that offered by thousands of independent businesses. The franchise contract is the key to everyone's success, and you must get used to its binding aspects early on.

This binding contract, which covers every conceivable point, creates a liaison between you and the franchisor that leaves little room for error of interpretation. Conflicts do arise, but they are less and less frequent now because of continuous refinement of franchise contracts. When conflicts do arise, they are most likely due to failure on the part of either party to appreciate fully that they are in business for a common end.

No two franchise contracts are the same, however. They vary just as the number of goods and services currently offered under franchise agreements varies widely and is expanding to this day. In some cases, contracts may specify the exact products and services that you may sell under the parent company's name, may dictate the hours and days of business, and may even specify in detail the types of uniforms that must be worn by participants.

You must question all the essential elements of the contract. If there are things omitted that you feel should be included, you must question that also. The contract is likely to be lengthy. Be on your guard against important clauses that are not set forth until the very end of the contract or that are couched in obtuse legal language. That is why we say repeatedly that you must have competent legal advice before you sign anything on the dotted line.

Your franchisor's most controversial "right," and the industry's big contractual hang-up today, is the so-called no similar business clause. This simply states that once you sign on the dotted line for a franchise, you cannot then become involved with any similar business. Usually, this limits you to a specific geographical area—say, a twenty-mile radius around your franchise establishment.

From the franchisor's standpoint, the no similar business clause prevents you from evading the royalty provisons of the franchise agreement. This clause does have some merit. After all, if you could open a similar but nonfranchised establishment under another name in a nearby area, you might obtain a large part of the benefit of what amounts to a second franchise without paying for it.

Not all aspects of the no similar business clause appear to have merit, however. Franchisors have made a fetish over trade secrets, claiming that the no similar business clause protects trade secrets. But, in my opinion, there are few real trade secrets today. Even patents can be evaded. Most of the time, so-called secret chemical formulas can easily be duplicated or broken down into identifiable components. If I were looking for a franchise for myself, the first mention of a secret formula would turn me off, perhaps permanently.

Franchisors do need weapons and protection. Your success

depends, on a large measure, upon the success of the franchisor. You must have ample justification for renouncing a franchise agreement. You cannot legally take down the sign that you buy or lease from the franchisor and put up another different sign for the same business. For this reason, the no similar business clause does lead to a high percentage of renewals after expiration of the original ten- or twenty-year franchise.

What should you look for in a franchise contract? The reliable Council of Better Business Bureaus, Washington, D.C., lists all points that are worth your study.

The first point involves a clear definition of your rights to sell or transfer ownership of the franchise. You want a clear understanding of this at the outset. You would not be likely to buy a major appliance or vehicle without first determining that you can get it serviced locally. The same principle applies in your franchise transfer rights. Study and understand them. When you "buy" a franchise, make sure you can "sell" it later.

Second, a description of the rights of your heirs or assignees in the event of death. You must consider all possible contingencies in a franchise contract. Death is not a happy thought, but you can be sure that your franchisor has long since considered this aspect and has acted accordingly. Protect your loved ones by understanding their recourse upon your demise—before you sign the contract.

Third, the classes of customers you can sell and the geographical limits of the territory in which you are authorized to sell. You want no surprises here after you have invested money and opened your doors. Military commanders do not attack until they are assured of full logistical support. Adopt their methods here.

Fourth, the nature and extent of your obligation to buy supplies from the franchisor or his approved sources. This has traditionally been one of the stickiest points between the franchise industry and government trustbusters. What you want is written assurance that you can purchase goods from the most reasonable source.

Fifth, your right to renew or extend the franchise beyond the original term of the contract. This has become a sticky point in recent years as some franchisors have found it desirable to run the units themselves, taking back the franchise upon its renewal if this can legally be done. You want to be sure that the option of renewal belongs to you.

Sixth, the rights of the franchisor to assign unpaid portions of the initial franchise fee to financial institutions or other "holders in due course." You might become involved with an uninvited third party unless you fully understand the contract terms.

Seventh, the "good clause" provisions under which the franchisor may terminate a contract. Obviously, there are some legitimate reasons for a franchisor to break the contract if there is clear negligence on your part. Such reasons should be clearly delineated in the contract.

Eighth, the terms and conditions under which you may terminate a contract. This is the opposite of point eight—the spelling out of the legitimate reasons why you may want out.

Ninth, the description of the exact training and support services that the franchisor is to provide you with. The extent of the training, the assistance you receive initially, and who pays these costs should be spelled out.

Tenth, a precise definition of the price, commissions, rental fees, and leases required to own and operate the franchise. There should be no ambiguities here, or escalator clauses, or hidden expenses.

Eleventh, the exclusive territory awarded to you. You want to be assured that such territory is exclusive as long as the franchise contract is in force.

One last point—take your time about signing the contract. A good franchisor is going to take his time so he can investigate your background thoroughly. You should do likewise. And under no circumstances should you allow a third party to act as a go-between. A franchise salesman or agent, working on commission, is apt to be in a hurry for selfish reasons. Forget about "middlemen" and deal only with company officials directly. This way haste cannot make waste.

Franchise companies get the bulk of their income from royalty fees and company-owned units. But a good slug of dough still comes from the sale of paper supplies, hardware and appliances, "secret" ingredients, and assorted other merchandise to you. It is this latter practice that is a bone of legal contention on contracts. The courts have decided that this practice of selling goods to you bears judicial review.

Until 1970, most franchise companies not only sold products and merchandise to their franchisees but compelled them to buy them. After a federal court ruling in a Chicken Delight case, companies struck the latter clause from their contracts, substituting a provision that the companies would offer to sell merchandise but would allow franchisees to buy outside if they followed stringent guidelines or bought supplies from a roster of approved suppliers.

In a case that has gargantuan implications, a few years ago an important decision was handed down in Pennsylvania, certifying a class action that included more than 1,000 Dunkin' Donuts franchisees, dating from 1955, and alleging tie-in claims relating to equipment, signs, real estate, and supplies. The court considered the granting of a franchise to be the tying item and necessary equipment, supplies, and real property to be the tied products. It held that it was an illegal tie-in violation for a company to "persuade or influence" franchisees to buy or lease equipment, supplies, or real estate from the franchisor or from designated sources.

Courts have previously held that the element of "coercion" is necessary to prove a tie-in. However, in this case, the court held that mere company policy to "influence decisions" was sufficient. The court felt that large franchise companies are able to throw their weight around due to sheer size. Dunkin' Donuts had 1977 total volume of $220 million. The jury reasoned that Dunkin' Donuts was possibly persuasive enough by itself to intimidate the small franchisee like yourself to buy from the company, even though it may be to your advantage to purchase from suppliers not on the company's approved list.

The fact is that size of the parent franchise company really has little to do with supply arrangements. Giant hamburger king McDonald's sells no supplies to its franchisees but instead issues quality standards that each unit must adhere to in order to keep its franchise. And we all know how well Ronald McDonald has achieved quality control. Other large franchisors require that only special ingredients be purchased from the parent.

As you might expect, the franchise industry has reacted angrily to the adverse court decisions. International Franchise Association, the industry's leading trade group, branded such decisions as "anticompetitive." IFA asserts that the ruling "in effect makes 'salesmenship' unlawful under the Sherman Anti-Trust Act." IFA envisions a rule of conduct that precludes a franchising company from offering what its franchisees may want, unless the parent is willing to accept the risk of treble damage liability for providing it.

I feel that the industry has a legitimate complaint against this decision. Quality control—a vital aspect of franchise agreements—must be maintained. Many salesmen, who travel by car habitually, have told me that they always stay at major national motel chain units because they know they consistently get the same quality accommodations at virtually the same price regardless of where they travel. I feel that the public feels the same way—they are drawn by the uniform quality, regardless of whether they are seeking quarter pounders, a dozen donuts, tool rental, or cleaning services.

From your standpoint, one of the big attractions in entering into a franchise agreement is that you are provided with supplies and other business aids that provide consistent quality and give you an edge on the competitor who goes it alone. If you cannot buy from your parent, how can you control quality and offer your product at a very competitive price?

Some experts admit that Dunkin' Donuts was perhaps slow

to adapt its tie-in arrangements to mollify legal eagles. So it is interesting to note that the company subsequently announced a new purchasing program, designed to enable franchisees to effect substantial savings and better cost control on an annual basis. The program enables those participating to purchase all Dunkin' Donuts-labeled products at fixed prices from a selected distributor for a one-year period. This distributor is selected by a regional committee elected by shop owners on the basis of markup, ability to service stores, and credit reliability.

Dunkin' Donuts' Distributor Commitment program is providing a cushion against shortages, is making cost forecasting more precise, cutting freight expenses, and generally making it possible for shop owners to program their business on a more stable basis. Products included in the program are doughnut mixes and fillings, coffee, and printed paper and packaging. The company says that advisory committees will maintain a continuing working relationship with chosen distributors. They try to coordinate the timing and amounts of purchases to assure maximum benefits from special situations, freight, and distribution arrangements. Ninety days before expiration of the yearly contracts, a new round of interviews is held to select distributors for the following year.

Now, it is true that Dunkin' Donuts is a special type of food franchise. If you own a unit of this type, you are affected by changing commodity prices. For instance, in 1974, sugar prices shot up to all-time record levels because of a combination of unusual circumstances. The new Distributor Commitment Program is apparently primarily earmarked to shield the small franchisee against suddenly soaring commodity costs. Of course, commodity prices could decline during the yearly contract, but the plan is designed so that the advantages clearly outweigh the disadvantages. The Distributor Commitment Program should also appeal to potential suppliers, since they too can look ahead annually, knowing that a contract will be in force.

This clearly represents a retrenchment from Dunkin' Donuts' previous tie-in arrangement. This program has obviated some legal objections while at the same time providing quality control so vital to your success. Such a plan also seems applicable to any other franchise line, since commodity costs are not the only ones that are rising. Inflation has taken its toll in terms of higher paper, ink, chemical, metal, and other costs.

The simple fact is that without quality control, your franchise agreement might become worthless. Quality control cannot be achieved without some sort of tie-in. Anytime the subject of tie-ins comes up, pay close attention to it.

The transfer of rights is another factor that is constantly in the franchisor's favor. Franchise rights are granted for varying periods. The term may be ten or twenty years, or longer. Some agreements are for only one year with the option of successive one-year renewals if both parties wish. Some terms may run for an indefinite length of time with a provision for cancellation by either party upon thirty to sixty days' notice.

Suppose that within the specified time limits, you decided you want to sell your franchise. In nearly every case, the franchisor has stipulated in the contract that he reserves the right to approve any transfer of the business. Admittedly, this gives him a great deal of leverage. The contract may well stipulate that in the case of transfer, you must furnish the franchisor with a general release of all claims against him regardless of substance and validity, you must pay him in full all debts owed, and that you must pay collection fees where the franchisor must initiate legal action to collect debts owed.

Goodwill can also be a sticky part of the transfer of a franchise. The value of goodwill is extremely difficult to estimate accurately. From your point of view, goodwill is derived from your own hard work and established reputation in the community. Your franchisor may, in turn, insist that goodwill stems from public acceptance of his products and trademarks. Thus, the franchisor may be able to force you to sell your franchise back to him for fair value less goodwill. The difference could amount to thousands of dollars.

5

Choosing a Good Location

Locating your prospective new franchise is awfully important. Hard work may pull you through, but location can be the difference between success and failure or between modest success and big success. Your franchisor will give you some help in choosing a good location. But he cannot do it all, and you must remember that he has a lot more money to lose than you have.

You must be aware that United States municipalities are becoming increasingly uptight over who opens what businesses where. And they are taking a dimmer view of thirty-foot-high, brilliantly lit signs necessary to attract highway traffic, or garish designs, or buildings that clash with the surroundings. In effect, local authorities are saying, "Have it our way," or not at all. Today, location could provide you with headaches that you never anticipated.

A good location for your small franchise, then, has to involve more than a good traffic count or expertly drawn lease.

Your franchisor will provide invaluable assistance in getting you going. But you, more than your franchisor, must live with and respect the rights of your neighbors.

There are physical and psychological aspects of your franchise that must be investigated before any deal is signed. Do not wait until after the opening, when your neighbors may unaccountably start bellowing about how your new operation is fouling up the visual aspects of the environs.

Of course, not all franchises have location problems. These headaches are largely centered on fast-food franchises or others where drive-in traffic is relied upon. Small franchises can succeed without being in the public eye or "under glass," so to speak. Some franchises can even be operated virtually from a home basement or garage. For instance, household cleaning services, which have been among the more successful small franchises, can be operated from an unobtrusive location that few neighbors would object to. However, a franchise business operated from a garage may soon require a warehouse facility for inventory. You must always keep expansion in mind.

Choice of franchise location depends upon many factors, such as vacancy of premises, nearness to your home, and familiarity with the neighborhood. Sometimes these factors appear all that is needed, and no further evaluation is necessary. This can be a mistake on your part. Will the area be bypassed by coming highway construction? Is the franchise that you are contemplating too specialized for the area? Are you going to offer something that is already adequately supplied by other businesses in the area? It makes no difference if the competition is a local nonfranchise operation. It is not likely to throw in the sponge just because you are about to cut the grand-opening ribbon. In fact, you can probably bet that the competition will become sharper and tougher because of your becoming the new boy on the block.

Franchise experts stress that you should like and be happy in your location. That is really a prerequisite. You should say *no* to an undesirable location that the franchisor tries to force on you. This is a psychological factor of no small import. Equally important is that you must make the franchisor prove to you that the community in which your franchise will be located *needs and will support your business.*

Locating a franchise is really a two-part exercise: (1) selecting the town or city, and (2) selecting the right specific site in a chosen area. In selecting the town or city, you should determine if the area population is still growing or has already matured or reached the peak of its development. Learn as much as possible about the composition of the population. A breakdown of residents by age, occupation, and income will tell you a lot. This may have a direct influence on your prospective sales volume. It may also have an effect on your full- or part-time employment supply. Learn something too about local high school graduates. Are they finding local employment, or do they have to relocate to move up the employment ladder? These can be important factors for your franchise.

You also want to pay close attention to the number of competitive businesses in your area. Do not take the franchisor's word as gospel. Dig around by yourself. Study Census Bureau, Chamber of Commerce, or local commercial bank statistics. Areas do become overstored and, when they do, casualties inevitably result. Statistics are not infallible, but most of the time it is foolish, if not disastrous, to buck them.

Of course, using your own intuition should not take a back seat in your selecting a location. There are intangibles such as community spirit that cannot be ignored. Do the people in the area cooperate fully in civic endeavors? What about church membership? Is it increasing or declining? This should shed some light on the civic zeal of the inhabitants.

Rely as much as possible on the opinions of experienced local authorities. If the area is going to change from rural to industrial, they should have a handle on this. If you are thinking of an industrial area, how well established is it? Is industry strike-prone? Long strikes could put you right in the middle. Also, try to determine if there is any threat of local industries moving away. Stability can be awfully important to the success of your franchise.

Several different types of locations are available within most cities or towns. These include the suburban location, shopping center, central shopping district, and neighborhood shopping area. First, the suburban location will draw customers from the local trading area. Operating costs and the level of competition here will depend upon the particular area.

A shopping center location for a franchise has a lot to recommend it. The shopping center has the advantage of drawing mutually beneficial trade into the center. Ample free parking is a big plus for this type of location, and you have an opportunity to benefit by participating in group store promotions. Balanced against this is the fact that operating and occupancy costs may be high.

Or the most desirable location for your franchise business may be the neighborhood shopping area. It draws potential customers from nearby residences, and it often offers the best break in occupancy costs since stores are usually smaller. Land acquisition costs or leases may also be cheaper. You should be able to provide more personalized service. Local taxes and insurance rates may also be lower. If not, however, this could outweigh all other favorable considerations. In contrast, the central shopping district may prove the least desirable for you. This location, which draws from the entire trading area, usually features high occupancy and operating costs. Competition may literally be right next door.

You can rely heavily on the economic status of the community that you are considering. For example, how does the number of telephone subscribers in the area compare with other comparable communities? The number of homeowners and the average property value are also illuminating. The age and make of automobiles owned by residents is also important. Bank loan and deposit statistics and average family income are other things that you should determine.

Not too much stress can be placed upon the ethnic aspects of your location. If you are a member of a minority group, this can be vital. Who knows the ethnic likes and dislikes of a neighborhood better than someone with a similar background? If you are not a member of a minority group but choose to operate in an ethnic neighborhood, make sure that your full- and part-time employees represent the dominant ethnic strain. They can help you.

Successful franchisees readily acknowledge that location is critical to success. One franchisee testified before the Federal Trade Commission in Washington not long ago that he had parlayed an initial franchise investment of $25,000 into a net worth of $2.5 million over a fifteen-year span. Another franchisee of the same firm testified that the company had no product specifications; therefore, location alone could have been the difference between success and failure in two similar operations.

Of course, if you obtain a really good location and do well there, you may eventually run into an unanticipated problem—the buy-back. Many locations have become "prize packages" to some large franchisors. They continue to aggressively buy back franchises when opportunities present themselves. Most franchisors have agreements that give them first option on any franchise that goes up for sale. In other words, you can retain the franchise until termination or until you decide to sell it. But in the latter instance, you can probably sell it only back to the franchisor.

Buy-backs are especially prevalent in big city locations. Franchisors reason that in the metropolitan areas, they obtain a density of store franchises that facilitates communication and management, plus distribution and marketing efficiencies. Statistics in the fast-food industry show that company-owned units outsell those operated by franchisees. So, be forewarned. If Papa Bear starts making noises about buying back your franchise, have your lawyer reread your contract to make certain what your rights are at that location. Upon franchise renewal, make sure that the same conditions as in the original franchise are included.

In locating a franchise, one must always be on the alert for changing trends. While a heavily trafficked suburban location would appear as Utopian, the winds of change may be blowing toward downtown again right at this moment. This possibility is worth examining, as it has several important ramifications. Not the least of these is that it may put minority group franchisees on their best competitive footing ever. The growing trend toward condominium living in center city areas creates captive clients for a broad range of franchised goods and services. Urban renewal has changed many a neighborhood's character virtually overnight.

As might be expected, the shrewd, aggressive fast-food franchisors are among the first to taste the nectar of downtown's rebirth. Kentucky Fried Chicken, A & W, and Dairy Queen are locating units downtown in increasing numbers. There are a number of reasons. In the suburbs, it is getting much tougher to find good highway locations. In a downtown location, the franchisee may need to draw customers from only a few block radius, whereas in the suburbs a two-square-mile radius may be required to make the business go. Downtown rentals run higher, but some operators find that they can get along with less space. If the downtown unit is located in a large building, it may be hooked into central heating and air-conditioning and exhaust systems. Also, a free-standing suburban unit may face soaring construction costs and real estate taxes. Downtown secondary locations can be had at a low cost per square foot because of tenant defections to newer high-rise buildings.

The energy crisis has had some effect on the downtown reawakening. In the past several years McDonald's has opened numerous units in shopping center malls and office buildings—including some in Manhattan itself. The *Wall Street Journal* reported that McDonald's was attempting to secure a location on an elegant corner on the upper East Side, and quite a "Mcfuror" developed. Eventually, Ronald McDonald won out. The hamburger chain is high on downtown locations because traffic on the nation's highways is down. One downtown Manhattan McDonald's did more business in one month than the first unit opened by the company did in a year.

Franchisors have done much to raise the level of business location to a high level. They can do a lot to put you on the right road. But you still must use your own guile and imagination. Make your own investigation of locations before you sign anything. You have nothing to lose but time. Then, in the unlikely event that you lose money, you have no one to blame but yourself.

6

Training—A Key to Success

Today, the independent small businessman faces two overwhelming obstacles in his path to success. One is the crunching competition of large, integrated companies and chains with their obvious advantages and economies of scale. The second is the continuing disturbingly high failure rate of independent, smaller businesses, particularly during the critical first year or two of existence. Going under early is usually the result of lack of management, capital, or operating skills. In short, many little guys run out of money and determination before they learn to compete successfully.

In franchising, the failure rate is low, and one excellent reason for this is *training*. As a prospective franchisee, you are not expected to have past business experience that will enable you to meet successfully new problems and new situations. The franchisor is selling his know-how and modern merchandising methods. He makes darn sure that you know the business from soup to nuts before you go on the firing line.

After that, he should offer invaluable continuing consultation services and help.

Franchise training is an intensive indoctrination, highlighting two weeks at the franchisor's home office. It is likely to be two weeks that you will long remember. You will be virtually shut off from the outside world as you sleep, eat, and drink your product and its merchandising. This training covers all facets of the franchise operation from bookkeeping to the dos and don'ts of servicing customers. In addition, most franchisors provide each new franchisee with practical field experience on the premises of an established outlet. The only way you could duplicate this as an independent would be through clandestine snooping—hardly a recommended business operating procedure.

Subjects included in home office franchise training programs normally cover a wide range of topics pertaining to the day-to-day specifics of the business. In addition to acquiring the basic knowledge and skills necessary to make, sell, or distribute the particular products or services, you will likely be instructed in record-keeping, inventory control, and insurance. Also, if you are going to employ other people in your franchise, you will need training in managing people. An experienced staff is an integral part of any business. You will want to know how to hire the best individuals for your business as well as how to train them for maximum performance in selling your franchised goods or services.

Franchisors today employ a number of techniques and devices to instruct you better. Teaching machines are coming into wide usage. Closed-circuit TV systems are proving very effective in that they allow trainees to witness their own mistakes through instant playback. Also, through prerecorded lessons, trainees are able to catch up if they miss a lesson. Recorded cassettes provide a "refresher" course for you should you fail to recall some facet of your intensive training indoctrination. In addition, franchisees can expect to receive during training sales and promotion material such as brochures, booklets, sales manuals, direct mail material, grand opening plans, signs, showcards, and so forth.

Here is how one substantial retail franchisor describes his training program in his introductory material: "Prior experience is not necessary. Franchises are granted on the basis of the applicant's ability to communicate, his stability, and his ability to manage others. He is enrolled in a four-week training program immediately prior to his store opening. A company Fieldman is assigned to his store for one week before opening to assist in merchandising, hiring and training personnel, and coordinating all prior opening procedures.

"The franchisee has a second Fieldman with him for one full week after opening for assistance in: training personnel, ordering merchandise, arranging credit sales, and getting the store functioning smoothly. A company Operations Manager is assigned to the franchisee for personal and telephone visitations in order to give him continuous counseling. Further, Fieldmen are also assigned to the franchisee for the purpose of maximizing sales, if needed.

"A merchandising man also visits the store monthly to assist in inventory, ordering, and in-store merchandising. The company's advertising agency creates TV films, radio tapes, and newspaper mats and places them for the franchisee in local media."

Perhaps the most important aspect of the foregoing is that the franchisor is there to help you all he can. After all, his purpose is to maximize sales, and the better trained you are, the more items you will sell. The franchisor will push you, but not in any crude manner like the old-fashioned slave driver type boss. Essentially, the franchisor pushes you by a program of planned, continuing educational assistance.

Besides home office training and help in the field, most franchisors offer important refresher training courses. This is a form of in-service training that can range from one-day seminars at the franchisor's home office to field-located sessions conducted by traveling supervisors. Many franchisors also conduct regional sales clinics at various times during the year. Such clinics are worthwhile because they offer you an opportunity to exchange views and discuss common problems directly.

What about the cost of this training? Some franchisors believe that you should pay your own living costs while you are undergoing your baptism of fire at the home office. In fact, some will use your willingness to assume that these one-time expenses represent a test of seriousness of purpose. Almost all franchisors require you to pay your own travel expenses to and from the home office training sessions, even though this may be a cross-country round-trip. Sometimes this cost can be included in your franchise fee, or you can pay it separately. A few franchisors will pay you a nominal salary to help defray your away-from-home expenses while you are at the home office.

In any case, the cost of training for you is really only a tree in the forest when you consider the implications of starting anew on the road to success. The franchisor makes sure that your "maiden voyage" is a success. He does this by sending a supervisor to look over your shoulder during the first critical weeks of your business opening at your location. These supervisors are also available to provide continuing assistance after you become established.

Although well meaning, some of this assistance may not be all it is cracked up to be. Sometimes, the assistance comes from area franchisees, who are literally paying off the franchisor for the privilege of (so-called) assisting others to open their businesses in a certain area. They may know little more than you do about charting a safe course on the seas of franchising.

It is also possible that the franchisor will send someone to assist you in the opening who is really there to set down strict rules that you must abide by. This individual's primary role may simply be to get you in line at the outset. It could be that such an exercise will simply reduce you to a subservient franchisee who is not likely to rock the boat with initiative. It will be up to you to determine how genuine this type of assistance really is.

Yet, there is no way that you should start your franchised business without benefit of comprehensive training. Make sure that all the training provisions are spelled out clearly in your contract before you sign. Although, obviously, training can vary widely depending on the type of franchise business you are entering, the following are generally found in the training programs of most franchisors:

A. On-site instruction provided at an established outlet of the franchisor. This outlet should have been in business for at least one year. Cost may be borne by the franchisor.

B. Formal instruction provided at a centralized training school.

C. Material for self-study provided by the franchisor. This type of training is particularly important in franchise businesses where sales ability and technique are prime requirements. Some franchisors will not accept you until such requirements are satisfied. This type of training is normally supplemented by regional meetings and seminars.

D. Periodic mailings such as house organs, bulletins, newsletters, and leaflets covering various phases of operations. These are particularly helpful since they generally include testimonials by other franchisees. You can learn much by the experience of others in overcoming operating problems and avoiding pitfalls. Any progressive franchisee should look for guidance in the experience of his fellow franchisees, particularly those who have been in business for a longer period of time. This is one of the best ways to increase your sales.

E. A detailed program of in-service training involving continuing assistance. Make sure that the franchisor won't drop you like a hot potato after the grand opening. You will need regular visits, say quarterly or semiannually, for the sake of continuity in developing your business. Training is a never-ending procedure.

Never take training for granted. I would go so far as to say that the difference in training might be the difference between one franchise opportunity or the other, particularly if they represent similar business opportunities. At the same time, be aware that some franchisees like to use the training period as more of an indoctrination so that you believe implicitly that what the home office says, goes. You want the franchisor's help but not his total domination. The training should strike a happy medium that should be discernable from reading the materials provided. Avoid unreasonable or oppressive franchisors by investigating before you invest.

7

Who's on Your Side?

As a prospective franchisee, you should be aware that during the early years of franchising, individual franchisees had little or no voice. Nearly everything said about the fast-growing field, which adds new franchises at something approaching a 50,000 annual rate, came from the franchisors. Without question, some franchisors have been good to their franchisees right from the start. But many have not. There have been numerous injustices, and this has led to frustration on the part of many individual operators. The views of franchisors and franchisees on certain issues were far apart.

Into this widening gulf has come the National Franchise Association Coalition, Wheeling, Illinois 60090, described as a "loosely knit but very dedicated group" of franchisees united in their goal of making franchisors more responsive to their needs and wishes. The impressive list of participating associations of franchisees with full NFAC membership currently includes: Ford Dealers' Alliance; International Federation of

Store Owners' Association (Dairy Queen); FACT (Council of Hertz Licensees); McDonald's Operators' Association; Consolidated Franchise Association (Dunkin' Donuts); American Association of Independent Newspapers Distributors; International Franchised Dealers' Association (Shakey's); National Baskin Robbins Store Owners' Association; National Beer Wholesalers' Association; Kentucky Fried Chicken National Association; Independent Dealers' Committee Dedicated to Action (auto dealers); Wine and Spirits Wholesalers of America; Midas Muffler Franchisee Association; National A & W Franchisee Association; and Denny's Franchise Owners' Association. The NFAC Associate membership lists also include various individual franchisees of many other systems and numerous other franchisee associations who have NFAC membership pending.

Fortunately, at about the same time in late 1975 that NFAC got off the ground at a Las Vegas meeting of representatives of twelve franchisee associations, legislation was proposed in Washington protecting franchisee interests for the first time. NFAC jumped at the chance to support the so-called Mikva Bill, which was subsequently voted down in the Ninety-fifth Congress. However, similar legislation is still pending in mid-1978.

The original Mikva Bill provided sorely needed protection against unjust terminations and failure to renew by franchisors. According to Jerry Waldie, NFAC legislative advocate in Washington, "The threat of termination or failure to renew hangs constantly over the franchisee's head. His independence as a businessman is dependent on the well wishes of the franchisor. His investment of time, work, and money is at the sole mercy of the franchisor. The franchisor too often uses that awesome power to compel action on the part of the franchisee against his—and his customers'—best interest."

NFAC told the writer that it believes firmly in quality control. It desires strong franchisors, but at the same time it also desires strong and dignified franchisees. It also desires better business relationships, better law, and ever improving social and economic situations for the independent franchised businessmen and the public at large.

It is remarkable that NFAC came to being in that it represents a permanent coalition of franchisees of all types and systems. Participants realized that franchisors almost without exception participate in their own trade associations. Thus, a coalition of franchisees was needed for the solution of common problems that affect all franchised businessmen beyond the realm of any single industry or any franchise system or any one trade group. With over 460,000 franchisees in the United States of all types, the potential for NFAC is obviously great.

With new franchisees coming into various systems all the time, these newcomers have been bumping into each other and into older established franchisees. The result has been a growing familiarity with each other's business, both within the same chains and between competing chains. Improved communications between various franchisees has made them aware that they share common problems.

The trouble with some franchisors is that for years they have believed that their franchisees were meek and naive. Many franchisor agreements read as if everyone operates in paradise. They read as if there is no reason in the world why independent franchisee associations would ever be formed. Yet NFAC Executive Director Gil Meisgeier, who is also head of the McDonald's Operators' Association, says that troubled franchisees cannot always take their problems or suggestions for improvements to the franchisor or his field representative for equitable discussion.

For instance, one southern McDonald's operator wrote the parent company that whereas at one time it seemed that the operator could do no wrong, the corporate thinking now is that the operator can do no right. The same operator noted that "we are paying annual service fees of $25,000 to $150,000 individually, depending on the number of stores operated. For this money we need help, not criticism. If we were retaining outside consultants for this amount of money, we would expect to be told what they were doing for us, not what we were going to be doing for them."

The McDonald's Operators' Association has three key principles and goals: (1) no operator should be summarily terminated, and each has the automatic right for renewal as long as company operating standards are maintained; (2) new units that cut into revenues of existing stores should never be opened; (3) McDonald's should pay for unit structural changes, except for interior improvements.

The McDonald's Operators' Association is regarded as one of the strongest of all franchisee groups; yet it numbers less than 20 percent of all McDonald's franchisees. This may be attributable to fear of reprisals from the parent franchisor. MOA claims that the parent company in the past has punished franchisees by terminating their franchises or not renewing them. The firm has also allegedly harassed the operator with frequent visits from quality control inspectors who cite the operator for small infractions and threaten to terminate him, or by not allowing them to open new units.

Naturally, the most successful and aggressive franchisee groups yet formed come mainly from the huge fast-food industry. This field has always been a leader in franchising. For instance, *Nation's Restaurant News* said some time ago that the Pizza Inns Franchise Association has been a model of effectiveness. Its membership represents 60 percent of the franchised Pizza Inn units. The parent pizza company quickly accepted the franchisee group and even publicized its formation in the chain's official operators publication. The group was formed primarily to give greater voice to franchisee opinions. The idea is that when the association brings an idea to the parent, the parent is sure to listen. If an individual tried the same tactic, the idea might fall on deaf ears.

One of the most widespread franchisee complaints is that once franchisors become publicly held, their outlook changes. The prime franchisor concern becomes earning profits and paying dividends to the public shareholders. Since the franchisor's royalty is skimmed from the top of gross sales, the franchisee often feels that he is pushed to the utmost to provide maximum gross sales, with little regard for net profit.

By the same token, franchisee groups say the quest for added sales volume upstairs hurts the individual's net profit. For instance, requiring franchisees to participate in various promotions by purchasing merchandising kits or couponing or offering price-off specials puts the pressure on the franchisee's profits. According to some franchise authorities, if such pressures result in a franchisee's failure, this can provide the franchisor with an opportunity to operate the business as a company-owned unit or to resell it at a profit as a "going business" to a new franchisee.

These pressures can arise from other sources. The Baskin-Robbins Franchisee Association complained that the franchisees are required to give away birthday ice cream cones free. This franchisor does not require royalties but instead makes its money from ice cream sales to operators. In effect, the franchisee must give away ice cream that he purchases from the parent company. The company may make money, but all the franchisee may get is heartburn.

The Statement of Principles of the McDonald's Operators' Association is very illuminating. It is reproduced below:

1. To the Franchisee, the McDonald Franchise is a valuable property right which becomes more valuable as it is being exercised by the Franchisee. This property right should not be arbitrarily terminated, and it includes a basic right of renewal which should not be arbitrarily denied to the Franchisee or to his heirs so long as their operation meets criteria set by reasonable and measurable standards.

2. In matters of renewals or expansion, business relations among the Owners of the Franchise should not be disturbed, so long as their operation meets criteria set by reasonable and measurable standards.

3. McDonald's announced policy of expansion based on criteria set by reasonable and measurable standards has become

part of each Franchisee's property right; therefore, it should be applied on a universal, non-discriminatory basis; and existing Franchisees in a market place, who are expandable, should be offered any new units which become available in such market place.

4. Encroachment in the market place of an existing Franchisee where such encroachment has a material, adverse effect on the revenues and earnings of such Franchisee is a violation of such Franchisee's property rights and should be discontinued.

5. McDonald's Corporation should assume the financial responsibility for structural changes and improvements. To the extent a Franchisee has paid for such structural changes and improvements, an equitable adjustment should be considered.

Consisting herewith, the Franchisee should continue to assume financial responsibility for all inside improvements; such as seating, fixtures, and equipment.

6. McDonald's should include in the original lease all items of lease hold improvements necessary and proper for conduct of business consistent with the high standards of McDonald's.

The National Franchise Association Coalition's Declaration of Purposes, while not exactly equal to the Bill of Rights of colonial independence days, was the first national declaration by which major groups of all types of franchisees stood up for their rights against franchisor interests. It is reproduced in its entirety below.

Whereas, the independent businessman has been the mainstay of a viable economy in a democratic society; and

Whereas, franchising has made it possible for many Americans to become and maintain themselves as successful independent businesspeople who benefit the franchisor, the franchise system, their employees, the manufacturer, the consumer and the public at large; and

Whereas, franchised businessmen in various industries have worked to develop high standards of product and service, on a regional and national basis; and

Whereas, the encouragement of the creation, growth, and strengthening of trade associations of franchised businessmen is in their best interests, their employees', the franchise systems' and the public they serve; and

Whereas, a coalition of franchised businesspeople is needed for solutions to problems which are regional or nationwide and which affect the public interest with an impact which transcends the bounds of one industry, one franchise system or one trade association;

Now, therefore, the National Franchise Association Coalition undertakes to organize as a coalition of independent organizations of franchisees and declares its purposes to be:

1. To promote, develop and maintain franchising as a viable mechanism for the continued development of independent businessmen to serve the public in a free enterprise system; and

2. To promote, develop and assist trade associations and other organizations of independent franchised businesspeople through communication and coordination with constructive action at all levels in this democratic society; and

3. To maintain research and education programs to benefit franchise systems; and

4. To work for, and assist franchisees in organizing and maintaining viable trade associations and organizations for independent franchised businesspeople; and

5. To coordinate and communicate with such associations and organizations for better business relationships, better law, and ever-improving social and economic framework for independent franchised businesspersons and the public at large.

Franchising's biggest hang-up is still the matter of disclosure. Any franchisor who selects a franchisee and then supplies him faces this problem. How much should he disclose? Riding to help your side now comes a knight in shining armor—the Federal Trade Commission. The FTC is the federal agency that has done most to help the embattled franchisees. It is committed to greater financial disclosure in franchise deals. If it is blocked from going down one road, it will find another. It matters not which side of the fence you are on. Painful as it may become, more financial information has to be disclosed in franchise agreements.

Over the years, the FTC has received a heavy volume of

complaints on franchise deals. These seem to fall roughly into three categories: (1) regarding services that the franchisor has promised to perform for the franchisee; (2) the profitability of being a franchisee; and (3) refundability of fees paid by a franchisee. Based on these complaints, the FTC is swinging into action.

Disclosure poses problems right from the word *go*. Those attractive, alluring franchise brochures sometimes cite profit projections that no existing franchisee has ever attained, the FTC claims. Sometimes profit projections are made before any franchises have been sold. In a survey of nearly fifty franchisors, the FTC found that many did not know what their franchisees' profits were. This was true of well-established and brand new franchisors. Exceeding actual experience in sales literature claims is one thing, but making claims that have absolutely no factual basis is quite another.

Little wonder that the Federal Trade Commission is currently considering trade regulations requiring full disclosure of all the facts that a prospective franchisee needs to make an intelligent, informed decision. There is no need for me to cite how high the stakes are. Committing a large part of your life, and life savings, to a venture created by others must be done on the soundest business base possible.

Disclosure problems start with the definition of a franchise, the FTC says. Some so-called franchise deals are so broad that they are indistinguishable from ordinary manufacturer-dealer contracts. Perhaps it would be better for everyone if some deals operated under a nonfranchise aegis altogether.

A problem that the FTC is currently wrestling with is whether or not the payment of a fee is a requisite for a franchise. This has been brought forcefully to light in connection with gasoline dealerships. Refiners have contended that there is no fee required, hence there is no franchise—simply an arrangement whereby one party agrees to sell the products of another. Gasoline dealers strongly contest this argument. They argue that a fee should not be made an essential part of the definition of a franchise. Further, they claim that even if the fee is an essential part, the alleged inflated tank-wagon price they had to pay constituted a fee, in effect. The argument goes that the gasoline dealer gets the benefit of the refiner's advertising, the use of his credit cards, and the use of his trade name. It would be a big help to all if the FTC can unravel this question of "to fee or not to fee."

At what point during the franchise negotiations should disclosures be made? From the prospective franchisee's point of view, disclosure should be made at the time of initial contact. However, franchisors hold that this is impractical, since a high percentage of inquiries are received from casual and insincere prospects. Why should they have to disclose valuable competitive information to tire kickers? But there is a point at which information should be disclosed. The FTC says most franchisors agree that from two to ten days before the signing of a contract is adequate.

What about an adequate cooling-off period following the signing of a franchise agreement? The FTC advocates a ten-day period during which the franchisee can back out if he chooses. Franchisors counter that if there is early disclosure before the signing, there is no need for a cooling-off period afterward. The point is that one or the other is essential for full understanding of or escape from the contract.

The most controversial point of all is the requirement that prospective franchisees be offered an opportunity to inspect the profit-and-loss statements of existing franchisees. Here, even the FTC admits, we tread softly into the confusing garden of confidential information, trade secrets, and perhaps even unobtainable information. It is hardly surprising that franchisors would object to giving out this sort of data. What is surprising to this observer is the FTC finding that the great majority of franchisees objected to giving out information about *their* individual profits. Moreover, the objectors offered few alternatives. The most common one is to furnish the aspiring franchisee with a list of names and addresses of area franchisees to whom they could go for information.

A related and controversial point is that of profit projections. Obviously, the sky cannot be the limit in projecting profits for starry-eyed fledgling franchisees. The FTC hopes to implement a rule that no profit projections are to be made unless they are based on the actual figures for non-company-owned franchisees during the preceding twelve months. This rule would be helpful as far as it goes. But what happens if no reliable figures are available at all? Aren't *no projections at all* less misleading than those of the pie-in-the-sky type?

It is important to understand that full disclosure at the appropriate time is not offered as a panacea for franchising's ills. No regulation or law is ever going to achieve that objective. The FTC knows this better than almost anyone else. Rules will not give businessmen good judgment. Rules won't give franchisees good judgment if they don't have any to start with. Rules cannot turn the unwary into the wise. Rules may not even cure the type of fraud that has bothered all forms of business from the Year One. But if rules make fraud more difficult to perpetrate and make it easier for the franchisee to understand what he is getting into, that is indeed laudable and desirable.

I have the feeling that franchisors and franchisees alike are too apprehensive about disclosure. I recall the furor a few years ago when the Securities and Exchange Commission made multidivision public companies disclose for the first time the contribution to sales and earnings made by each division. The multidivision companies fought bitterly against disclosing this information mainly because they did not wish to disclose which units were carrying the freight and which were the weak sisters. Now, such information is commonly made public, and I fail to see that any harm has befallen those affected by the change. In the same breath, I fail to see where greater disclosure on the part of *both* franchisors and franchisees can harm the industry.

One innovative practice to be applauded is the growing

number of franchisors using some form of franchisee advisory organization to improve communications and understanding. This represents a conscious effort to decentralize authority and involve a maximum number of people in decision making. In the strong food-service industry alone, there are nearly two dozen IFA members who now have franchisee advisory councils. Of these, a very high percentage believe the council program improves communications and relations between the company and its franchisees. The councils were also deemed helpful in operations, marketing, and advertising.

In view of the above, you should look for a franchisor who consults with you regularly on various matters. The more you hear from him, the stronger will be your bond and the less will be the opportunity for friction. Unfortunately, through no fault of your franchisor, the antitrust laws do not permit this contact in the widest possible latitude.

As a prospective franchisee, you may well want to see if there is a franchisee association in the field that interests you. For while franchisors and franchisees must not fight pitched battles, the operators' associations are here to stay, have growing support in Washington, and will make more and more waves just as the union labor movement did at its inception one hundred years ago. This is all to your advantage as a small businessman. You need all the help you can get. There are more people on your side than ever before.

8

Promoting and Advertising a Franchise

No man is an island. Thus, prospective franchisees must constantly keep in mind the fact that franchising's own success has placed growing demands upon its operatives. In the eyes of the public, franchising has arrived. It is solid and respectable and gaining ground all the time, except perhaps in the eyes of the environmentalists, who see the proliferation of fast-food shops as evil personified. On the whole, though, the public sees the McDonald's, the Dairy Queens, and the AAMCO's as solvent, well-run businesses. They realize that both the franchisor and the franchisee are solidly entrenched on a plateau of respectability.

What is so great about being a respected franchisee? An independent businessman might occupy the same niche, but it would likely take him much longer and, of course, his clientele would likely be much smaller. There is no way the small independent can achieve the stability implied by a franchisee backed by an aggressive, powerful national franchise organization. Unless the independent is a "one-of-a-kind operator," the public will tend to look upon him with some innate fear that he may stumble and fall along his business "way" at some point in time. To be blunt about it, in this highly competitive age, most people fear for the competitive life of the independent.

In franchising, you most likely will be representing on a local basis a large national organization whose advertising is probably known to many through media exposure. The success syndrome of franchising has some implications that you may not have considered. They are not anything that might make you change your mind about entering the field. All the same, you may discover that, just as movie stars shun the public eye, you should be on another planet or in another line of endeavor. The franchisee is in the local public eye constantly.

Perhaps the most surprising aspect of this limelight thrown upon franchising is that the demands upon your time may not be centered just in the operation of the business. No franchise will work by itself, no matter how clever the home office is. You know from the excellent franchisor training provided that you are going to have to spend a large number of hours each week in the conduct of the business itself.

But have you thought about the extracurricular demands on your time and effort? This is usually a surprise, if not a shock, to the small franchisee or independent businessman. Then, too, these demands are almost always coupled with demands for monetary assistance. The success that we mentioned earlier has resulted in a connotation of being able to give substantially in the eyes of the public. The implication is that if you are the local cornerstone of a national franchise, you must have spare cash hanging about. So you will be called upon to support some organizations that you never knew existed. They literally come out of the woodwork seeking donations once your franchise is rolling.

Because you have to get involved with the community in

which your franchise operation is located, the problem should be dealt with swiftly. No national franchisor is screwy enough to tell you to sit back and wait for business to break down your doors. You must make friends and create goodwill for your business. In a word, you must promote.

The best way to promote your business is through community involvement. While this takes time, it can have some advantages. For instance, it can help develop your business personality. This sets you apart from other local businessmen. You become known around town as a fellow who spends little time on the seat of his pants. You become known as a worker.

Community involvement begins with a few basic tenets. First, you should studiously avoid doing anything that is potentially harmful to your community. Beat the drum for and boost your surroundings at every possible opportunity. You must never upset your neighbors by allowing undue noise, smoke, or odors to run rampant. Schedule deliveries so they do not create traffic hazards or block sidewalks. If you violate any of these no-nos, the resultant adverse publicity can hurt your business more than you ever believed possible.

The "open house" may seem like a king-sized headache, but it is really a time-tested, effective means of starting a franchise business off on the right foot. This is nothing more than inviting your neighbors in for friendly socializing. However, some new franchisees tend to let the friendliness that pervades the open house slip after this event is over. This is a mistake. You can create an open house atmosphere all year around. You can repeat it on each anniversary or even on other occasions, such as completion of expanded facilities, refurbishing, or anniversaries.

Another very effective means of involvement is to offer your premises as a site for community meetings after working hours. This can help attract new people to your franchise business. Be sure to invite local school groups to tour your facilities. If you can, provide them with some sort of token free gift while there. Kids—your customers of tomorrow—

remember these things. Also, sponsoring local youth teams and groups creates instant goodwill.

Along similar lines, it is a good idea also to offer your premises to local fund-raising groups. You know they are out there, and they always need and seek help. They will publicize you by publicizing themselves. Offer your paved parking lot for off-hours fund-raising events such as car washes, selling chances, or signing pledges. You may develop more future customers this way than by any other more expensive means of promotion.

Of course, you can overdo involvement just like anything else. Some new franchisees try to take an active role in too many local organizations. As a result they are too busy to rise to leadership in any one group. It is better to choose one active organization and really work hard at making your role in it successful. Such a course of action often leads to committee positions and eventual leadership. After your term of high office is completed, you might then become involved with another organization and go through the same procedures. In this way you will gain the lasting respect of the community.

Community involvement means being a good neighbor. If your franchise involves large display windows, these can be used effectively to promote such local civic organizations as the Rotary Club, Kiwanis, war veterans, or Boy Scouts. Stay on the alert for tie-in promotions during "National Clean-up Week" or the United Fund Drive. Photos of local high school sports teams are regarded as very effective in gaining attention from parents.

You will have to budget your time and money in civic endeavor. You cannot give more time or money than you can afford without hurting yourself. Your franchisor will be the first to notice this, and it is a safe bet that he will let you know about it. You must set aside funds for civic activities gradually. They do not properly come from the advertising-promotion budget for your business. This is a public relations or goodwill expense. It should be based on your past contributions and your current level of profits.

Other local businessmen may be able to give you advice on charitable spending. Local meetings or conventions provide a good means of "talking shop" on this point. Communities with active chambers of commerce often publish guidelines on such subjects for the guidance of members, franchised or not.

Guarding against the unforeseen and unexpected charity donation is not easy. You can help yourself, however, by making it known that all requests must be received by a certain date. Total up the requests and look over your own results to see if the requests are exorbitant. Or you can set aside a fixed figure in advance and then allocate donations from it. Either way, you will have established a control over a most sensitive issue.

Another thing—exercise some care over how your charity dollars are used. If you give your children money, you want to know what they are going to do with the money. The same principle should apply to charitable organizations. Ask them what they are going to do with the dough. Too often, only a small percentage of a charity donation goes for the cause itself. The rest may go toward supporting ballooning administrative expenses. For this reason, a donation through a central organization is a good idea. Let your donation be channeled to various worthwhile charities. Make sure that requests for donations are formal, in writing, and are filed away for your income tax returns. This file will also help you plan future donations.

Bear in mind that no franchisee can operate in a vacuum— without friends or goodwill. Neighbors are your best customers, and it is hoped that they will be good friends. You need them. Proper community involvement is the best way to ensure a harmonious relationship that will last down through the years. You will profit from this, and so will your community.

In addition to promotion, the kind of advertising done by

you, and your franchisor, is of great importance to the success of your franchise. No small business can succeed without some advertising expense, but the question is often, "How much is enough?" Many businessmen have a mental block about advertising. They believe that they cannot afford to advertise or that they are unable to tell if their advertising dollars do any good. You must avoid such mistakes when starting out a new small franchise.

Every franchised business needs to advertise, regardless of whether it is testing the market water or is an established business. In fact, one of the salient things about the franchise industry is that large franchisors, practically without exception, have long since learned that they must develop a national brand image through advertising, promotion, and public relations programs. This is an obligation owed by the franchisor to every unit in the system. The biggest thing you have going for you locally is your franchisor's carefully cultivated national image.

When a franchise agreement is signed, you can assume that the franchisor will continue to promote his brand name. He expects you to protect this image. Thus, advertising becomes an integral part of the package deal. You have a responsibility as a potential investor to study the franchise contract to see what is said about your obligations to the franchisor regarding use of his brand name. This powerful marketing asset must be properly used. The low industrywide failure rate in franchising can be largely attributed to a shrewdly developed advertising and promotion program in which both the franchisor and you participate.

Franchise advertising programs vary widely, depending upon the nature of the business and how long the franchisor has been in business. They may also vary in cost. Usually, the agreement provides that the franchisee shall be subject to an advertising fee in an amount equal to 3 percent of the franchisee's gross sales per week, or to a maximum weekly dollar figure, whichever is higher. And usually, a majority of the franchisees must contribute to the cooperative advertising pool in order to make it operative.

Most reputable franchisors have effective advertising programs covering radio and television, national magazines, local newspapers, and sales promotion. Typically, the franchisor will prepare a packaged promotional campaign that includes direct mail material, point-of-sale display material and signs, highway signs, leaflets, handbills, newspaper mats, and house organs. It is up to you to avail yourself of as little or as much of this material as you need.

Even before your franchise unit is open for business, the franchisor is making preparations for advertising your business. You can expect to be given a wide range of publicity releases and materials for announcing the opening of your business. During your training at national headquarters, many ideas such as contests and other promotions will be discussed.

In newspaper advertising, you may expect to receive a paid opening newspaper advertising campaign complete with all the professional trimmings. You will also receive from time to time various news releases that may be placed in local newspapers as free publicity. Designed to complement your advertising, such interesting and timely news stories will cover your grand opening, poster contests, etc. These are usually prepared by experienced advertising and public relations personnel to stimulate community interest and generate additional sales volume.

Most franchisors take full advantage of the often overlooked medium of radio advertising. This medium is particularly effective in selling franchised services to businessmen, especially those who keep their car radios on while traveling or driving to and from the office. Many radio stations offering quality programming at reasonable advertising rates are used to profitable advantage. Usually, professionally prepared radio commercial scripts are included in franchise advertising packages.

Direct mail is one of the most powerful advertising tools of all. This method has been time-tested as an effective low-cost method of generating continuous year-round business. You can expect to be provided with a series of professionally designed and written sales letters and brochures. These should provide both new and repeat business. All areas are covered, including mailing lists, postage rates, timing, maintenance, circular distribution, and so forth.

Telephone solicitation can be one of the most effective and least costly means of promoting additional business for you. Your franchisor will show you how you may generate hundreds of dollars worth of additional business each month by following carefully prepared telephone solicitation scripts. You should be counseled step-by-step concerning the most responsive business categories to approach by phone, the best times to call, and how to arrange for local housewives to make your calls from their homes. It is possible that the franchisor will be able to provide all this without incurring any significant additional telephone bill charges.

Franchisors who direct their advertising exclusively to the national market feel strongly that all local franchisees should get equal coverage. Since you and all the other franchisees are paying the same fee for advertising, regional advertising is unfair to the contributor outside of that region. Some, however, still believe that advertising must be composed of three elements—national, regional, and local. They hold that each coverage fortifies the other.

Some franchisors have regional advertising bases wherein an advertising agency contracts to carry out a program for each major region. But local advertising is really the foundation for all franchisors and franchisees. Most of the time, the franchisee is encouraged to "tie-in" local advertising with the national campaigns of the franchisor. For instance, if a franchisor is advertising a product nationally, the local franchisee is encouraged to advertise the same product, along with a "buy it here" theme.

A growing and constructive practice is for franchisors to start advertising committees composed of various local franchisees, who meet regularly to discuss where and how advertising funds should be allocated. This provides a give-and-take forum wherein you, the franchisee, can present ideas that may be widely adopted by your franchisor. Such committees are governed by franchisees themselves. Regional and district sales meetings often have provisions for discussions of advertising programs.

One of the most favored forms of advertising for franchisees is optimum use of the telephone directory Yellow Pages. This usually involves at least a boldface listing or, preferably, a plain listing along with a sizable rectangular ad that gives details on the product or service supplied, hours of opening, and alternate telephone numbers to call in off-hour periods. Many Yellow Pages' ads also pinpoint the business location through use of a small area map showing main thoroughfares. This is especially helpful in obtaining transient business from motels and hotels.

Advertising funds can be collected in a variety of ways. Before you sign any franchise agreement, be absolutely clear in your own mind how this works. Advertising will help your franchise, but you want as few surprises starting out as are possible. The first few weeks and months of operation are the toughest in any business because of unforeseen costs and adversities. An advertising hang-up should not be one of these.

Some franchisors require their franchisees to spend a percentage of yearly gross sales in a local advertising program. Remember that this could be in addition to what you may be required to contribute to any national cooperative advertising costs. In some cases, your advertising cost may be included with your continuing royalty payments. You or your attorney should check this out.

Grand-opening advertising expenses are normally covered by an extra amount charged in the franchise sale price. This can be so many cents per unit or a part of the rental fee at retail, for example. In a large franchise chain with thousands of franchisees, what may appear to be a very small sum to you may amount to millions of dollars for the franchisor to spend on powerful national advertising to benefit all the participants.

Of course, the franchisor cannot do it all for you. You will have to use your ingenuity to some extent in local promotion and advertising. You should know which local newspaper or medium will get you the most mileage from an advertisement or the most coverage for a publicity story.

The main thing that the franchisor will want to get across to you is that he always retains ownership rights to the brand name of the franchised product or service. You will be required to display this brand name prominently as well as advertising it in a prescribed, approved manner. Before you sign a contract, it is a good idea to talk with other area franchisees, particularly those that have been in business for one year or more. Ask them if they are getting their money's worth from advertising contracts with the franchisor.

In sum, before you sign anything, you want to know how much you will be paying for advertising. Will you have a say in how your money is spent? What area is covered by the franchisor's marketing and advertising program? How much leeway is provided you in terms of local advertising campaigns? Is the help that the franchisor will provide spelled out clearly?

Examine your franchise contract closely. You are given a reasonable amount of time to do this before you have to decide in the affirmative or negative. Remember that there are two sides to franchise advertising, and both parties have responsibilities. The franchisor's responsibility is to provide a good product that is adroitly advertised and promoted. In turn, you are required to provide good service to the product. If he meets the first two requirements and you meet the third, you have a deal that should be mutually beneficial.

9

Proper Record Keeping and Accounting

The toughest part of franchise failure is that nine times out of ten it involves people who are far from wealthy to begin with. Unfortunately, many of the franchise opportunities with the highest success ratios—such as McDonald's and Holiday Inns—also cost the most to obtain. If a franchise costs over $100,000, it is normally out of the reach of the average individual. Conversely, some of the lowest priced franchises have been the least successful. Taking it on the chin all too often is the little guy with a few thousand dollars of spare cash but little more in reserve.

Franchising is the last place in the world for the gullible individual. Advertising today is often clever and potent. Sometimes, stars of the sports or entertainment world are used to promote franchises. The testimonials of luminaries are small comfort to those small investors "psyched" by such glowing praise.

Your best defense against coming a cropper in some ill-founded franchise scheme is sound financial advice. You should retain the services of a local accountant before you sign a franchise agreement. You need someone who not only possesses the experience and practical know-how in every aspect of a small franchise business but also knows local business conditions. This accountant should come from a small firm rather than a large one. A large firm probably would not be able to assign the type of accountant you need for a fee that you can afford to pay.

You undoubtedly will do plenty of talking to your accountant, but you should also do plenty of listening. If the accountant is really sharp, he should be able to steer you away from many poor franchise buys. He should be able to see right through those transparent profit claims. He should be able to take apart those alluring projections of operating profits with sales, cost of sales, gross profits, operating expenses, and net profits laid out so convincingly. Accountants are inherently mistrustful of figures—as they should be. Their livelihood depends upon numbers.

Unfortunately, too many franchisees never achieve the profits promised in the franchisor's glowing brochures. Sometimes, long hours of hard work plus a large capital investment fail to add up to a decent return. Why? First and foremost, the profit goals may have been overly optimistic in the first place. If you are behind the eight ball at the start, there may not be enough elasticity in the business to make adjustments. Second, there may have been insufficient time for the business to reach its full potential. Third, unexpectedly lower profit margins may have been caused by poor management. This management factor may be a problem for either the franchisor or the individual franchisee. If the franchisor is expanding too rapidly, he may be obliged to raise fees and prices to offset lower profits. This is the reverse of what you as a potential franchisee are entitled to think should be the case.

Information disseminated by the franchisor tends to be very general—too general, in many instances. Specific information is often lacking on the total investment required and how the investment is financed. This is why you should retain a competent accountant before you make any moves.

One thing you must watch carefully is whether or not you will be the first, or one of the first, franchisee operating in a given area. If this is the case, the distribution system may be strained by the lack of proximity to headquarters. Inventory and supply orders may have to be placed far earlier than you would like, and the time gap may make it next to impossible for you to approximate your requirements accurately.

Critical to good record keeping and accounting is an understanding of cash flow. Cash flow is simply the estimate of capital that will be necessary in order to put the business in operation, including payment of current bills and buying inventory. After that, even if the business is profitable, you may still run out of money. A positive cash flow is vital to any business.

Something should be said here about the size of the franchise investment. Franchises come in all sizes from huge to piddling. The huge franchise is generally beyond the financial scope of the ma and pa team. These are largely for investors— people with large sums of money available for investment, perhaps in multiple units of the franchise. The investor rarely does any work. He just watches over his investment, deriving current income and tax advantages.

At the other end of the spectrum is the franchise that requires only a few thousand dollars investment. This may be the most appealing opportunity for you, but it may also be the most deceiving. In the first place, you should be suspicious of a very small dollar investment franchise because it may not be a franchise at all but rather a simple distributorship. Under the latter arrangement, you will be supplied with a product, but you are strictly on your own from there.

Remember that small-scale businesses seldom produce profits that are out of proportion to their size. It is virtually one chance in a million when a small investment and a small-scale business produce large dollar profits. Generally speaking, the profits of any business are relative to the scope and size of the business itself. Wild claims of profits are likely to lead to trouble for both you and the franchisor. Nearly all small business bankruptcies over the years have resulted from poor business management. The biggest pitfalls historically have been (1) poor financial planning because of inadequate records; (2) poor sales management or market analysis; (3) poor administration and expense control; and (4) neglect in all phases of the business.

A good place to start in these important determinations of franchise worth is in sales volume. Say the franchisor projects $1,500 per week in your prospective franchise business. What does this mean? What is this projection based on? Is it drawn from comparisons with similar outlets in comparable locations? Can the franchisor supply you with copies of the certified statements used to document the profitability of the early franchisors (those with the longest operating experience)? Such statements would be very important to your accountant in determining sales and profits or losses.

Another thing about sales that you and your accountant should investigate is this: Does the $1,500 weekly level take into account any "break-in" period, or do they expect you to start out at top speed? You must learn if there is a seasonal aspect to your franchise. Can you sell $1,500 worth of goods or services every week of the year? Or does the $1,500 mean that this is what you can expect for only 30 weeks or so. If this is the case, then total volume may be considerably short of the annual gross that you might have supposed by multiplying $1,500 by fifty-two weeks.

Cost of sales is also vital and is often underestimated by the neophyte. Your accountant should be able to help you immeasurably in determining how much price stability there is locally with whatever supplies are involved in your prospective venture. The franchisor may not have used current prices.

In any case, you must avoid figuring profits on the basis of cost of sales that is too low.

Operating expenses are difficult to project, but they are, likewise, pivotal. Both you and your accountant must make a detailed study of all anticipated expenses. You should apply both cost of sales and expenses to sales volume for a projected period in order to arrive at a reliable profit estimate. Labor costs are usually the largest operating expense, often running as high as 50 percent of all expenses.

Your accountant can help you calculate a most important statistic—your daily average sale. If your daily average franchise sale is $2.00, then you need to make 750 sales per week, or about 11 sales per hour for a seventy-hour week. Is this reasonable in your proposed business? Can you and your workers handle such a work load? And do not overlook fringe labor costs such as unemployment insurance, social security, and so forth. Can you actually hire help in your area for the wages projected by your franchisor? There are potential booby traps here that will likely require outside help.

There are other important operating expenses that may be beyond your control. Take rental expense, for example. Is this figure likely to rise? If the landlord's real estate taxes increase, this will likely be passed on in the form of higher rent. You will have to leave some leeway here, and your accountant should have some valuable advice.

The cost of utilities has shot skyward since the energy crisis. These costs used to be taken for granted in business operation, but no longer. Double check any estimates along these lines. Ask the local utility for cost estimates based on your operating plans. Also, ask neighboring businesses what their average utility costs are. Here, again, the good local accountant should know his way around. His fee will be well worth it.

Experienced franchisees will tell you that even after you have figured all your possible costs, it may be wise to add another 10 percent for contingencies. These can involve such things as the cost of uniform rental or the cost of maintaining rest rooms, parking areas, and so forth. Trash must be collected, and such service is seldom free. Innocuous expenses add up. Watch them.

Underestimating costs can be troublesome in other areas as well. Little things such as promotional brochures or place cards can be amazingly expensive to design, print, and distribute. If you underestimate your labor costs, this means that your payroll taxes withheld may be sub par. Insurance is another area where you will likely need help. Then, there are things that you might never anticipate. For example, if the weather is bad, your snow removal expenses may be heavy. Have you taken that into consideration? Also, you should be prepared for a steady stream of requests for donations to the local little leagues, United Fund, and various service organizations. You cannot meet these demands from petty cash.

Operating profit is another category where you will probably need your accountant's help. Perhaps you can achieve the objectives outlined by your franchisor but only with you and the members of your family working endlessly in the business. Could you work for someone else in a nonfranchise business, work fewer hours, receive valuable fringe benefits, and come out with the same income? On the other hand, perhaps you are the type of individual who would never be happy unless you were your own boss. If the latter is the case, this is something that neither you nor your accountant can really put a dollar value on. Franchising has allowed many persons to become their own boss at relatively little capital outlay and with a high likelihood of success.

Projected sales volume is at the top of your income statement for good reason. This is critical. If other projections prove fairly accurate but sales projections by your franchisor prove unrealistically high, particularly during the first year, you are in trouble. You and your accountant will have to visualize things realistically and on a long-term basis. What lies down the road in terms of sales? Can you physically handle projected increased sales volume?

Record keeping is mirrorlike. It does not lie. Keep it simple. Make it adaptable to day-by-day computations. Keep it so that it requires only a minimum of your valuable time to make daily or weekly entries. And lastly, keep your record keeping in the hands of a local accountant. He is the best person outside your business to tell you whether things are going right—or wrong.

10

Insuring Your Business Premises

One of the most important aspects of franchising is also one of the least emphasized—exposure to and insurance against loss. To be sure, your parent franchisor provides you with plenty of help, as indicated in earlier chapters. The franchisor does a lot to put you on the right track. But when it comes to insurance, the situation is still confusing.

You need insurance, and you should consider this vital aspect of running a franchise business profitably before you make any commitments whatsoever—particularly before you sign any agreements. Do not wait, friend, until after you have signed the agreement or even until the first day you throw open your doors, hoping that the public will venture in. You can risk your entire investment by not having insurance against the many perils that can befall you and your business.

Before you sign anything, you need to know what the risks are, what coverage you should seek to protect you against these risks, and how much this coverage is going to cost. If

you plan to operate a franchise within a central city neighborhood, for instance, your insurance exposures might be severe,
and you can figure that the cost of coverage will be high. The
potential for violence, in which you might be only an unlucky
bystander, is there. You may not be able to obtain insurance
that would limit your loss to a reasonable level in a firebomb-
ing or robbery. Insurance companies will back away if the
potential for serious loss is high.

Most franchisors will try to find you a location far enough
from high-risk areas so that you can obtain insurance at
reasonable cost. Many have established insurance programs on
a group basis. The insurance companies like this, as it is
much easier for them to spread risks based on the experience
of many individual businesses rather than dealing with you
one-on-one. Find out if the franchisor has a property/casualty
insurance program available at the first personal meeting or
soon thereafter. It is worth making a separate inquiry about
this factor alone.

The basic types of insurance are fire insurance, business
interruption insurance, casualty insurance including workmen's compensation, and business life insurance. Fire insurance and the related lines of insurance against windstorm,
tornado, explosion, riot, aircraft, and so forth provide protection for the physical property of your franchise.

The coinsurance clause in an insurance contract regulates
the minimum coverage necessary on your building and con-
tents before the company will assume all of the risk in any
loss covered by your policy.

The main thing to keep in mind with regard to fire
insurance is that your property should be properly appraised
so that it is insured for its full insurable value. Once you have
fire insurance, it is equally important to reexamine it periodically to make sure it covers your property at current value. In
other words, some allowance should be made for continuing
inflation in terms of replacement cost. Many insurance companies recommend adding a certain percentage to the coverage
each year. This may result in higher premiums, but it also

provides realistic coverage in today's terms, not those of five or ten years ago.

Business interruption insurance reimburses you both for the loss of profits and for fixed expenses if you have to shut down your franchise business because of serious damage from fire, tornado, hurricane, windstorm, or any of the insured perils.

Casualty insurance includes a variety of coverages. Of course, automobile insurance—both collision and public liability—is a major field of casualty insurance. Casualty insurance also includes protection against loss resulting from such crimes as burglary (or forcible entry), robbery, theft, or larceny. The latter would exist, for instance, when a person enters an unlocked door in your establishment and makes off with your property. Casualty insurance also includes plate glass insurance and health and accident insurance.

Liability policies are particularly important to you because of potentially huge losses that could result from third-party claims. Franchisors are generally scared half to death by the possibility of being held responsible for damage claims stemming from actions by franchisees. Such claims may come about when third parties believe that dealer operations are either field units of the franchisor or are agency establishments of the franchisor. As a result of this, franchise contracts often stress that the franchisee is an independent contractor and not the agent or employee of the franchisor. To protect himself against third-party claims, the franchisor usually stipulates that you may use his name only in certain specific ways. You may also be required to name the franchisor as an insured party in your liability coverage.

An important aspect of casualty insurance is workmen's compensation insurance, which protects your employees against loss resulting from job-connected accidents and certain types of occupational illness. As a rule, you will be required by state law to carry workmen's compensation insurance for your employees.

Business life insurance provides necessary protection for a franchise business or for the family of the businessman. After all, uninsured loss could occur because of the death of someone associated with the business. Such coverage is invaluable and will help keep the business continuous for your family. Among the numerous types of this coverage is keyman life insurance, which reimburses for loss upon the death of a key employee. Partnership life insurance retires a partner's interest upon his death. Corporation life insurance retires a shareholder's interest upon his death. Proprietorship life insurance provides for maintenance of the business upon the death of a sole proprietor. Another form of business life insurance is insurance to aid a firm's credit status. In other words, it covers the owner or key man during the period of a loan or the duration of a mortgage.

Fidelity and surety insurance is concerned with your employees and others with whom you deal. This type of insurance protects you against their possible dishonesty. Employees occupying positions of trust in handling company funds are usually bonded as protection against their dishonesty. Surety bonds protect one firm against the failure of another firm or an individual fulfulling a contractual obligation.

Credit life insurance is also important and related to the above, in a sense. Credit insurance protects businesses from abnormal debt losses such as those resulting from a customer firm's insolvency due to tornado, flood, recession, or other factors. And title insurance is an important factor in the purchase of real estate. This insures the acquisition of a clear title by the buyer.

In obtaining proper insurance protection, you should cover the largest loss exposure first. Be sure that on property coverage, valuations are sufficient and liability coverage limits are high enough. How can you know this? One reliable way is to check current awards by local courts in insurance cases. Your coverage should be acquired only for major potential losses.

It is a good idea to use deductibles wherever they are applicable. Various policies may be placed on a three- or five-year basis and staggered as to date of premium payment. Every possible means of finding ways to reduce the cost of insurance should be exhausted. Transfer of risk is a method worth investigating. Here, you can transfer the risk or loss from auto accidents by leasing the vehicle instead of purchasing it. In that way, the lessor is responsible for maintaining the insurance. It is quite likely that the lessor can obtain significantly lower rates than you can.

You will need enough insurance to protect against major losses but not necessarily against every little loss. This is something you must judge for yourself. The main thing is to be able to afford reasonable coverage. If you feel that the expense of insurance is too high for the amount of business that you project for your franchise business, then perhaps the best course is for you to forget the prospective business venture. The franchise cannot be worth the investment necessary if you cannot afford the proper insurance.

Fortunately, a few large insurance companies are starting to offer insurance programs specifically designed for groups of typical franchisees. Because insurance policies vary by state to some degree, and prices vary by territories within states as well as by state, the final product delivered will be adjusted to local requirements and state regulations.

You should find and use a qualified local insurance agent. This may not be as easy as it sounds. There are agents and then there are agents. But if you ask your lawyer, accountant, and so forth to suggest a competent agent, you can get a lot of valuable assistance in plowing through the insurance problems.

In addition, the needs and desires of individual franchise businesses are somewhat different. Of course, you as an individual franchise business owner cannot go individually to an insurance company and expect to get preferred treatment. But groups of franchisees can do this now.

Franchisees of a particular parent company have many similar exposures to loss. This means that large insurance companies such as Marketdyne Int'l Division of INA Corp., Philadelphia, Pennsylvania, and Famex Division of Fireman's Fund American Insurance Companies, San Francisco, California, offer valuable services. They develop not only insurance recommendations but loss-control services as well. These companies work with groups of franchisees and also approach the individual franchisor. Transactions are carried out by local insurance agents in any case. You should find this method preferable and worthwhile.

The above large insurance companies can help you meet your risk requirements under the Federal Occupational Safety and Health Act. This is very important. Reduction of risk through careful attention to loss control is a major responsibility of every business today.

To provide broad protection for franchisee groups, these insurance firms offer package policies. Various forms of property and liability insurance, formerly written as separate coverages, or as pick-and-choose selections with separate limits, are combined into a single policy. This virtually eliminates any complicated selection and overlap of coverages and limits. You merely select two limits—the replacement cost value of your building and the actual cash value of your business personal property. Nearly every other coverage feature is automatic. A simplified rating procedure enables a company agent to prepare a quotation quickly.

Franchise business owners' policies provide business liability protection and automatic business income loss protection (including necessary payroll expense) for up to a specified number of months (depending upon the type of policy purchased) if the business is damaged by an insured peril and cannot operate.

Your business can be protected against: fire and lightning; extended coverage, which includes windstorm and hail; explosion (excluding steam boilers); riots; riots attending a strike and civil commotion; damage by aircraft and vehicles not owned by the operator or a tenant of the premises; smoke from other than industrial or agricultural operations; vandalism and malicious mischief; sprinkler leakage; building glass and signs; and certain transportation perils.

Even more comprehensive "all risks" coverage is available. "All risks" means that all direct physical loss of or damage to the insured property is covered, except as specifically excluded in the policy. Such coverage is subject to only a few common exclusions, such as unexplained or mysterious disappearance, wear and tear, freezing, flood, landslide, credit default, false pretense, and so forth.

Business personal property is covered under new insurance policies for its actual cash value (up to the amount of insurance purchased) with no coinsurance. For seasonal franchise businesses, special peak season coverage is available that automatically increases the amount of insurance substantially to provide additional protection for seasonal variations.

Business personal property protects personal property used in your franchise business, including stock, furniture, fixtures, and equipment while on your premises. Also included are money and other negotiable instruments on your premises or in a bank, including some monetary losses while you are en route off premises. Other aspects covered by the business owners include: (1) business personal property at other locations for up to thirty days; (2) the property of others in your custody while on your premises; (3) your business personal property and the property of others while in due course of transit within 100 miles of your premises for pickup and delivery; and (4) Tenants' Improvements and Betterments.

Other optional coverages available include optional exterior glass coverage, which provides "all risks" coverage on all exterior glass, including frames and lettering, subject to certain specific exclusions. This coverage is on a replacement-cost basis. Optional exterior signs coverage applies to signs under buildings or business personal property. Glass coverage is automatically included when buildings are covered and you wish to cover exterior glass for which you are responsible.

Tenants' fire legal liability is an optional coverage that protects you for your legal liability for fire damage to premises leased by you.

Business owners' policies are available in most states for a large variety of franchise businesses through organized groups. They do not protect loss expenses from the operation of automobiles or liability under workmen's compensation and employers' liability laws. Such coverage must be provided under other policies.

Both Marketdyne and Famex have carried this concept a step farther by adding a group dividend factor. In other words, they help the franchise group form, in effect, their own insurance company by carefully separating their experience as a group and sharing the profit, if any, with them in the form of dividends. Dividends, which cannot be guaranteed in advance, are payable only after declaration by the insurance company's board of directors from surplus accumulated from premiums on policies subject to dividends. This dividend feature does not apply to employee benefit programs and applies only in states where permitted by law. Dividends are in the form of a percentage of the individual member's premium and are returned, unless otherwise arranged, to the individual members. Marketdyne, for example, had more than 220 groups, which paid $151 million in premiums in 1978. Some $6 million was returned in the form of dividends.

Marketdyne stresses that it is a marketing company that serves as the link between the insured group and the underwriting company. It does not handle the insurance transaction. The local franchisee does that with his local agent. Marketdyne does the advertising, mailings, trade shows, and publicity to increase membership awareness of the availability of the group (safety group) programs. Meanwhile, Famex operates the same way using over 225 professional insurance agencies around the country.

An obvious question arises: If franchise operations exist,

basically, to provide economies of scale such as centralized purchasing and marketing and advertising support due to their franchise affiliation, why can't they do the same for their property and liability insurance needs? You cannot act alone, obviously. But working with local or regional franchisee groups, you should find out more about what these companies (and others that are likely to join in over a period of time) can offer. For more information, write to Marketdyne International, Inc., P.O. Box 7725, Philadelphia, Pennsylvania 19101 (telephone 215-241-2935), or Famex, 3333 California Street, San Francisco, California 94119 (telephone 415-929-2117).

11

Franchises for Minority Group Members

There can be little question that franchising offers prospective minority businessmen untold advantages over developing a business independently. Franchising gets you over those high walls that keep you separated from success in business. It provides capital, training, and continuing assistance. These are things that have in the past been denied blacks and other minorities because of deep-rooted job discrimination. Franchising brings to the minority franchisee business expertise and knowledge that is vital to his survival.

The fledgling white businessman has many doors open to him. He usually has little difficulty obtaining funds from banks, finance companies, the government, or from well-heeled relatives and friends. This is a primary reason why the white businessman is usually successful, provided he makes the other sacrifices necessary for success. The sources of capital also can provide good financial advice.

On the other hand, blacks and Hispanics usually get a cold

shoulder from banks and finance companies. Their friends and relatives are no help because they normally do not have money to lend them. Thus, their ambition is too frequently crushed before it gets off the ground.

Geography is also no help to the aspiring minority group businessman. Most of the small businesses in ethnic neighborhoods are white-owned by people who do not live in the neighborhood. They do business and bank their money elsewhere. However, this drawback is not fatal. Such barriers are slowly crumbling—thanks partly to the powerful assistance of strong national franchisors. With such help, the minority businessman can, indeed, exploit the advantage of intimate knowledge of the neighborhood, its habits, and traits.

A strong national franchise can succeed anywhere, even in a low-income ethnic neighborhood. The basic concept of a franchise is to offer goods and services at very low cost through mass buying and standardized facilities. Fast-food franchises, such as McDonald's, Kentucky Fried Chicken, Chicken Delight, All-Pro Chicken, and others have operated successfully in poor neighborhoods. Ice cream shops and convenience food stores are other food areas where franchisors have been successful in ethnic neighborhoods.

In my opinion, there are still many areas of franchising that have not been fully exploited either by black or Hispanic franchisees or by being located in ethnic neighborhoods. They include: auto rentals, maintenance and cleaning services, travel bureaus, tax preparations, copying services, training schools, auto transmission and brake repair, paint and hardware stores, laundry and dry cleaning, temporary help, construction and remodeling, burglar- and fire-alarm installation, and car washes.

Suppose you find one of the above franchises applicable to your own needs? Your franchisor should help you a good way up the capital ladder. Many franchisors offer ample financial assistance to you. Since his own reputation is at stake, he will make a strong effort to see that you operate successfully and profitably. If your franchisor does not provide all the capital needed, you can turn to other sources, starting with the nonprofit Interracial Council for Business Opportunity, with main offices at 470 Park Avenue, New York, New York 10016. This organization has a staff of qualified professionals in banking and finance to help you.

If you are not averse to red tape, you can turn to the government for assistance. If you are a veteran, you may be eligible for a GI loan from a local bank with the aid of the Veterans Administration. GI loans are available for buying a business, buying land or a building for business purposes, purchasing business supplies, and a host of other legitimate business needs.

Government reports offer continuing hope for aspiring franchisees from minority groups. The Department of Commerce feels that the chief reasons for the popularity of franchises among minorities are that they help overcome inexperience in business and management and inadequate financing. Franchisors usually offer minorities managerial training and continuing assistance and financing for necessary equipment. The franchisor may also arrange for property leases, SBA loans, and loans from local banks and may participate in the venture himself.

Data collected from 1,166 respondents to a recent USDC survey show that in 1976 nearly 400 franchisors had a total of 4,300 franchises owned by minority businessmen. This compares with 346 franchisors with 3,400 minority franchisees in 1975 and 340 franchisors with 3,072 minority franchisees in 1974. Many franchisors, however, still do not keep records clearly identifying minority franchisees.

Of the 4,300 minority-owned establishments, some 1,900 were owned by blacks, 1,500 by Hispanics, 770 by Orientals, and 135 by American Indians. Many minority-owned businesses are concentrated in these fields: auto products and services, fast foods, food retailing other than convenience stores, 508 in convenience stores, and 223 in construction, home improvement, maintenance, and cleaning services.

The trend toward downtown locations should mean tremendous opportunities for aspirants who are members of minority groups. After all, who knows the ethnic likes and dislikes of a neighborhood or block better than someone who has actually lived there and shopped there? And certainly the minority franchisee should receive more worthwhile assistance—financial and otherwise—than ever before. This should help overcome the long-standing obstacles that have largely kept minorities from taking advantage of this new way of doing business.

The reasons that minority groups have not participated in franchising are not hard to find. Department of Commerce studies have cited these obstacles: (1) lack of experience, (2) lack of business orientation, and (3) difficulty in borrowing money. For these reasons, minority-owned businesses have thus far been concentrated in the popular franchising sectors of automotive products and service establishments, food stores, and fast-food restaurants.

Since the minority group member is more prone to failure in any business venture, the advantages of a franchising deal should be much greater. These advantages include centralized purchasing, standardized operating methods, inestimable assistance in picking locations, management training, continuing management counseling, company advertising, and financial assistance.

Minorities should not expect lenders to adopt a no-questions-asked attitude. They will require that you obtain an adequate amount and a proper mix of equity capital, debt capital, and credit. To obtain debt capital, which takes precedence over the other types in any liquidation, you must have in hand sufficient assets to obtain a loan. To accumulate such assets you must have equity or seed money—an investment in your business that shows that you mean business. You also need credit to balance your cash flow during periods when your obligations exceed your receipts.

Government lenders can come down pretty hard on you. This is because, traditionally, the risk of early loss in minority business is very high. Of course, if you show the backing of a national franchisor, your chances are much better for obtaining more than a minimum amount of capital. Generally speaking, the federal government Small Business Administration provides debt capital, while the MESBICS provide the necessary equity capital.

Government efforts to help you obtain capital have been abetted by professional organizations and organizations in private business. Such organizations include the National Association of Accountants, American Institute of Certified Public Accountants, and the Federal Government Accountant Association. Trade associations such as the Menswear Retailers Association and the International Council of Shopping Centers continue to be helpful.

Two chief reasons why minorities have shied away from business are (1) a general mistrust or unfamiliarity with the business world, and (2) a big disadvantage in geography. "Few ghettos have decent and successful businesses in them from which young people can learn good business practice," comments Brady Keys, Jr., president of All-Pro Enterprises, Inc., one of the most successful minority-owned franchisors of fried chicken outlets. Keys stresses that franchising combats these deficiencies by bringing to the minority franchisee business expertise and knowledge that are vital to his survival.

When it comes to capital, franchising helps the aspiring minority member even more. Says Brady Keys, "Franchising brings valuable assistance to the minority franchisee through proven financial planning and assistance in accounting procedures. It can even assist in the initial financing of a franchise through deferred payments and other advantages."

More important, perhaps, to the minority franchisee is the assistance that various government and public sector organizations can provide. In fact, Brady Keys feels that government assistance is the key to developing minority business success. His own firm, the nation's largest black-owned-and-operated fast-food chain, has benefited from this assistance. Some of these agencies that offer assistance are: Economic Development Administration (EDA), Office of Minority Business Enterprise (OMBE), Small Business Administration (SBA), and Department of Commerce Minority Enterprise Small Business Investment Corporations (MESBICS).

There are currently 97 MESBICS operating across the country. Only about four MESBICS, of which the most active is believed to be that of Burger King, are in the franchising industry. The others are Cottman Transmission, Convenient Food Stores, and Swiss Colony Stores. The U.S. Department of Commerce Office of Minority Business Enterprise estimates that at least half of all the MESBICS have made one or more franchise investments. A list of MESBICS and other organizations that fund minority businesses may be obtained by writing the above organization, Washington, D.C. 20230.

Another potent source of financial assistance for minority franchisees is the nation's 82 minority-owned banks. These banks, located primarily in urban centers, currently have total assets of $1.8 billion. A number of these banks have indicated an interest in working with franchisors and MESBICS in the development of franchise businesses in their marketing areas.

Unquestionably, OMBE has helped break down a lot of barriers confronting minority franchisees. The new businessman must obtain both an adequate amount and a proper mix of equity capital, debt capital, and credit. To borrow debt capital, you must have in hand sufficient assets to secure a loan. To accumulate those assets, you need equity or seed capital—in other words, investments in your business. You also need credit to balance cash flow during periods when obligations exceed receipts.

Unquestionably, lenders have come down hard on the new small businessman. Financial institutions consider both the cost of administering minority business investments and the risk of early loss to be very high. Traditionally, they have refused to provide more than a minimum amount of capital, and then only on a short-term, secured basis. As previously mentioned, usually the federal government Small Business Administration provides debt capital, while the MESBICS provide the equity capital.

Government efforts to help the minority businessman have also been bolstered by professional organizations and associations in the private sector that have the manpower, knowledge, and experience necessary to provide substantial levels of assistance. The willingness of private sector organizations to support minority enterprise programs has been amply demonstrated. More must be done, however.

The auto industry has been a leader in providing franchise opportunities. General Motors, for example, has enrolled numerous minority dealers in an eighteen-month training course. Almost two dozen oil companies supporting the minority business effort are striving for parity in service station ownership. Private sector business and trade associations such as the Menswear Retailers Association and the International Council of Shopping Centers continue to produce minority business opportunities. Other vital services to minority businessmen are being provided by the National Association of Accountants, the American Institute of Certified Public Accountants, and the Federal Government Accountants Association.

Also, OMBE offers relatively modest supplements to the budgets of traditional educational institutions to stimulate management development training. Introductory courses in business management are being offered at about forty different institutions as a result.

As Brady Keys opines, there is a lot left to be done by these groups, but they have already accomplished a great deal. "It is safe to say that without such assistance, All-Pro would not have developed to the extent that it has today." His advice to potential minority franchisees is simple: "Get all the help you can." This means consulting the above agencies and others, looking at various opportunities within the franchising field, and talking facts with minority franchisees already in business. Brady Keys stresses the latter, because his company has made some mistakes to go along with the successes. However, the company has profited greatly from its experiences and freely gives advice, particularly to those entering the fast-food franchising. "A potential minority that has his eye on a particular franchise business would be doing himself a disservice if he did not seek out the advice and knowledge of existing minority businessmen," states Mr. Keys.

Because of the greater adversity faced, the minority franchisee is more likely to make early mistakes—which may slow growth for a time. Brady Keys's very successful All-Pro Chicken organization made mistakes along the road to success and freely admits this. For this reason, Mr. Keys stresses that a potential minority franchisee should avoid signing anything until he talks with several minority franchisees already operating in the line of business in question. Success in business today is fraught with pitfalls. Not even a strong national franchisee can guarantee minorities that they will avoid all of them.

12

Franchises for Women

In the last four years, the number of women owning their own businesses has more than doubled to 978,000. Yet few of these businesses are franchises. Thus, the purpose of this chapter will be to investigate the tremendous opportunities existing in the unique franchise field for women as the march toward equal rights inexorably continues.

First, let us look at where female business owners are making the greatest inroads and, later, how this drive may affect franchising in the future. A study completed by Esmark, Inc., a diversified Chicago-based company with major interests in many areas, found that more and more women are starting their own businesses today. Their objective? "To find work in a tight job market, freer expression of creative and management abilities and to personalize their notions of how the business world should operate," said Esmark.

Esmark figures show that in 1972, there were some 400,000 women-owned businesses generating nearly $10 million in receipts in the United States. Now, female entrepreneurs are nearing the one million mark, with at least twice 1972's dollar revenues to show for their labors. Well over half of the women who own businesses (61 percent) operate apparel or accessory stores or sell general merchandise. Another 13 percent run restaurants or bars, and 11 percent operate beauty shops, laundries, dressmaking services, and child care facilities. The median age for women business owners in the retail trades is forty-four. Of course, numerous female business owners are professionals or creative artists, but they have little bearing on this discussion.

In addition to women owning their own businesses of varying types, there exist a tremendous pool of potential franchise operators from the huge and growing number of women in the labor force. According to the Women's Bureau of the United States Department of Labor, there were over 37 million women in the civilian labor force, and they were of all ages from sixteen to seventy in 1975. During the last fifty-five years, the ranks of women workers have risen from only one out of every five to two out of every five workers. More importantly, over this period of time the profile of the average woman worker has changed greatly—from that of the twenty-eight-year-old single factory worker or clerk of 1920 to that of the thirty-five-year-old woman of today who may be found in any of a great number of occupations.

Women have accounted for nearly three-fifths of the increase in the civilian labor force in recent years. They have supplied many of the workers needed for expanding industries— particularly the service-producing industries, where their contribution is required for the continuing functioning of health, education, and other vital areas. They are also making inroads into occupations of a more nontraditional nature.

In 1975 (latest figures available), 46 percent of all women sixteen years of age and older were in the labor force, compared with only 34 percent in the early 1930s. Although women are most likely to be working if they are young, have no children, and have completed their schooling (eighteen to twenty-four years old), their rate of participation is also relatively high and consistent (about 55 percent in the so-called prime working years of twenty-five to fifty-four). In fact, the greatest gains in labor force rates since 1950 have been registered among women twenty to fifty-four years of age. Women are least likely to be in the labor force if they are under eighteen or over fifty-four years of age.

According to the Women's Bureau, about one-eighth of all women workers are of minority races. Their labor force participation rates are generally higher than those of white women. Some 49 percent of all minority women were in the labor force in 1975, compared with only 46 percent of white women. Among women of the usual working ages (eighteen to sixty-four), the respective proportions were 56 percent and 54 percent. Minority women constitute almost 46 percent of all minority workers. Thus, opportunities for minority women in franchising may be substantial.

Women are more apt than men to be white-collar workers, although the jobs they hold are usually less skilled and pay less than those of men. Women represent 20 percent of all professional and technical workers, with teachers and health workers accounting for the lion's share. Women account for 72 percent of all teachers (except at the college level) and 64 percent of all health workers. Only about one-fifth of all managers and administrators are women. By contrast, nearly 80 percent of all clerical workers are women. However, there are more than four million women secretaries, stenographers, and typists who have a very good knowledge of the businesses in which they are involved. The writer suspects that there are many capable women secretaries who really run businesses while their bosses are in absentia for numerous reasons.

The Women's Bureau feels that women should enjoy opportunities in selected professional and technical, managerial, clerical, skilled craft, and service occupations. In addition, legislation prohibiting sex discrimination in employment will continue to open up new opportunities for women to train for and enter into more diversified jobs and to advance to jobs of higher skill level. Women who are well-informed about opportunities before making career selections will be able to capitalize on these opportunities in fields where skilled workers will be in demand. Still other factors pointing to continuing increases in the labor force participation of women include advances in the educational attainment of women in particular fields, greater longevity of women, plus the trend toward smaller families.

When researching women's role in franchising, this writer was amazed to find virtually no statistics on the subject. The United States Department of Commerce, which regularly issues its voluminous reports on the impact of franchising on the economy, does not break down its occupational data by male and female. And the United States Department of Labor's 1975 *Handbook on Women Workers* does not even mention franchising in its 400-page text or 14-page index.

Of course, there are plenty of females who work for franchisees, particularly behind the counters of fast-food franchise operations. And there are some husband-and-wife teams, such as Bonnie and Bill LeVine of Postal Instant Press. But in most instances, the female is largely subservient to the male leader.

It seems inevitable to this observer that women will make a much larger mark in franchising over a period of time. Actually, there would appear to be very few types of franchises where women could not manage successfully on a par with males. Physical endurance would seem to be the only drawback in some instances.

Conversely, there are many types of franchises that would appear to be very applicable to female management and operation. They include: accounting and tax services, advertising services, art galleries, auto rentals, beauty salons, beauty services, cosmetics, business services, candy stores, credit and collection services, donut shops, employment agencies and personnel, food shops, restaurants, health aids and services, home services, ice cream stores, laundry and dry cleaning stores, women's clothing and specialty shops, pet stores and services, schools, sports and recreation, and travel agencies. There are already many franchises under the above headings, but few, as yet, are run by females.

The paucity of female franchisees is not the result of any conspiracy. Franchisors these days must bend over backward to avoid being tagged as discriminatory. They are increasingly seeking out qualified minority group applicants (as discussed in Chapter 11). No franchisor with all his marbles would want to be accused of favoring male franchise applicants over female ones. So the answer to this riddle is perhaps that women have just not gotten around to applying for franchises to any large extent. This is bound to change.

Esmark, in its study of women in business, lists some effective factors for success that certainly apply to franchise aspirants of the female gender. It comments, "A well thought business plan is essential to success. Such a plan ought to encompass an outline of the product—how and where it is to be manufactured and at what cost, with an assessment of competition and consumer interest. Devising a marketing strategy is near the top in starter priorities for new women's businesses." (It should be noted that in franchising, the marketing strategy is pretty much established by the franchisor.)

Esmark stresses that profit-and-loss statements and cash flow projections should be prepared for a minimum of three years, and preferably five years, to allow female entrepreneurs to meaningfully gauge their capital needs. This writer heartily concurs with Esmark in any female aspirant's lining up professional services at the outset. Most potential businesses, whether run by a male or female, require a lawyer, accountant, banker, and insurance agent.

Esmark also suggests that organization charts of staff and duty lists be drawn up. These should be helpful to employers and prospective clients. They will also help outside counsel in figuring cash-flow projections. A further helpful suggestion by Esmark is that the potential growth of the business should always be made on three sets of sales assumptions—low, expected, and better than expected. By this means, risk and reward potential is included in any evaluations.

One mistake that a female potential franchisee may make is to expect free advice or free service because she is a member of the so-called weaker sex. This is decidedly unprofessional. In order to be thought of in the same terms as male franchisees, you should expect to do things the same way as male-run operations.

A female franchisee should expect to have the same problems and initial setbacks that any male-run franchise would. It is important for the woman franchisee not to be discouraged by initial lack of success. As long as you do not become overextended financially, you should surmount the critical first months of business. To forestall problems, and ascertain when and how much cash will be on hand in your business, a monthly cash flow is desirable.

And, of course, you have to trust your own judgment just as any male franchisee would. As Esmark put it so well, "Become used to personal assertiveness under stress." In fact, says the female businesswomen study, "Know thyself" is the best preliminary exercise for the potential entrepreneur—and one that will dominate the future success of any business.

Female franchise aspirants can obtain help outside of that furnished by the franchisors themselves from the Small Business Administration or from the International Franchise Association, the leading trade organization, both located in Washington, D.C. Over a period of time, the barriers to success in franchising should become fewer and lower. Who knows, maybe even in a few years, someone will bother to issue statistics on women franchise managers. This would be one important sign that females have *arrived* in the land of franchising.

13

Best Franchise Opportunities

The latest "explosion" in franchise growth involves the business of franchised real estate brokerage offices. Companies such as Century 21 are emerging as new franchise giants. Expansion in this field should continue rapidly for the next few years, providing both independent real estate brokers and persons seeking to enter the industry with three big advantages: (1) an immediate nationwide image, (2) complete nationwide advertising, and (3) an efficient interbroker referral service on a national scale.

This is a highlight finding of *Franchising in the Economy, 1976-77,* issued by the Industry and Trade Administration of the U.S. Department of Commerce. Real estate franchises are lumped into a Miscellaneous Business Services category that also includes background music, business, engineering and marketing consultants, and others. An estimated 13,600 such establishments will be operating in 1978, up from 11,400 in 1977. Sales will top $1 billion in 1978 for the first time. The report estimates that there will be 13,400 such businesses owned by franchisees and only 200 company owned. This represents a 20 percent gain over the number of franchisee-owned businesses in this category in 1977.

The report also anticipates that fast-food restaurants will maintain their leadership role in franchising. It also warns that much of this growth will be at the expense of grocery stores and supermarkets. Currently, one out of every three food dollars is being spent eating out, and the ratio may rise to one of every two food dollars in the 1980s. You should consider this carefully if you are thinking about acquiring a convenience store or other food-store franchise. You may be able to combat this trend by offering more carry-out operations of your own. However, there are plenty of opportunities in such promising fields as campgrounds, instant printing, real estate, rustproofing, water conditioning, and weight control.

Campgrounds

Today's fast-growing campgrounds industry represents a blend of a Holiday Inn and quiet wilderness. Peace and quiet is harder and harder to find. Our forefather pioneers found it hard to escape, but today's pioneer uses the motor home, travel trailer, tent trailer, and van to find real tranquillity. It is hardly surprising then that camping has become the fourth largest sports activity in the United States. Camping's over 60 million enthusiasts are topped only by swimmers, bicyclers, and fishermen.

Campgrounds represent an attractive alternative to the expensive hotel-motel route. It is also less confining. AAA estimates that nearly $100 per day is required for a family of four to travel in the United States. By using franchised campground facilities, Americans can get by on less than half of the above amount.

Higher gasoline prices are not keeping Americans from camping, however. The recreational vehicle industry forecasts

725,000 RV shipments to dealers by 1980. Canadian RV production is also showing a strong growth pattern. Total RV ownership in North America is expected to reach nearly ten million units by 1980. In addition, more than one million tents are sold in North America each year.

Franchised campground operators can look for substantial dollar volume increases. Median family income is predicted to reach $18,000 by 1985, while the average work week will be reduced to thirty-four hours. Also by 1985, outlays for leisure activities are projected to rise by more than 100 percent to $280 billion annually.

The campgrounds industry stresses that camping is no longer just a summer activity. People camp out year round as the urge to return to nature increases. Also, smog is a growing year-round problem. Many Americans travel in all four seasons. This is creating a shortage of good camp sites and a growing opportunity for franchised campground operators. Federal and state governments are placing increasing restrictions on land use. This means that private enterprise must provide additional facilities for the camping devotees. Incidentally, Kampgrounds of America, the largest franchised operator, has more camp sites than the U.S. Forest Service and Park Services combined.

Industry officials note that while an individual might be able to build a pleasant, efficient campground on his own, it is virtually impossible for him to promote it as the nationally franchised operators do. These firms effectively utilize such means as road signs, painted bulletins, paper billboards, newspaper and magazine ads, camping directories, travel show exhibits, movies, color brochures, caravans, and advertising specialties. Many testimonials are on file showing over 100 percent increase in business following franchising. Some report increases in camper nights double what is anticipated.

Franchised campground operators are also in a better position to provide you with potential income from sources other than campsite rentals. Convenience store operation is cited as a top revenue producer. Other money-making adjuncts include laundry rooms, game rooms, miniature golf courses, trout ponds, paddle boats, and horse rentals. Training, often on college campuses, is extensive and detailed, covering such vital topics as site selection, zoning approval, purchasing property, building permits, sewage treatment, bookkeeping and accounting, swimming pool operation, insurance, and other facets.

Franchised campgrounds operated by such leaders as Kampgrounds of America, Jellystone Campgrounds Ltd., and Safari Campgrounds are achieving the same aura of respectability that the fast-food leaders have. The "built-in" advantage of franchised facilities scores points that are hard to beat.

Kampgrounds of America

Kampgrounds of America is the outgrowth of a single, privately owned campground in Billings, Montana. It is now the largest franchised operator—in fact, it believes that it is larger than all of its franchised competitors combined. KOA operates over 800 grounds in the United States, Canada, and Mexico.

KOA facilities differ substantially. Some have as few as 50 campsites, while others have more than 500. Some are located adjacent to interstate highways and other primary roads for overnight business. Many are far back in the countryside and are more like resorts. All offer free hot showers, clean rest rooms, swimming, laundry facilities, convenience stores, playgrounds, and many other camper comforts. Fees run from $4.00 to $15.00 per night.

According to Harold C. Lloyd, vice president of sales for KOA, the franchise is purchased in two payments of $7,000 each. The first payment is made upon application and the second when construction begins (normally within one year of application). Average cost of a KOA campground is from $100,000 to $200,000. Estimated cost of a seventy-five-site KOA is $120,000, excluding land. Bank loans for 65 percent to 75 percent should be available, depending upon the franchisee's net worth. Thus, the franchisee may have to put up only about 30 percent of the cost. Recommended operating hours are 7A.M to 10 P.M., seven days per week, but exact hours and season are set by the franchisee.

For further information, contact Mr. Lloyd by writing Kampgrounds of America, Inc., P.O. Box 30558, Billings, Montana 59114, or phone 406-248-7444.

Jellystone Campgrounds Ltd.

Jellystone Campgrounds Ltd. is under exclusive license by Screen Gems, Inc., a subsidiary of Columbia Pictures Industries. This provides exclusive access to the "Yogi Bear" cartoon character of Hanna-Barbera Productions. Campgrounds are known as Yogi Bear-Jellystone Park Campgrounds. A vast array of Yogi merchandise is offered in the General Store, Gift Shop, Goodies Shop, and other areas of the park.

Jellystone Campgrounds prides itself on being extremely selective in picking franchisees. Some fifty-two parks are in operation in twenty states and Canada. The franchisor wants to build a quality park image and therefore has moved slowly to develop the system.

Jellystone franchises cost $15,000, payable in installments. Some $9,000 is due upon signing the franchise and the remainder upon commencement of construction. A royalty and service fee of 3 percent of gross receipts from the sale of campers and recreational vehicles and 6 percent from all other operations is payable annually. Since 1975, Jellystone franchisees have been able to offer an exclusive line of travel trailers, which, the company states, provide profit margins of $1,200 to $1,600 per unit. Dealerships to handle the Jellystone travel trailer line are automatically part of a campground franchise at no extra cost.

For further information, contact J. E. Webb, Vice President-

Marketing, Jellystone Campgrounds Ltd., 236 Michigan Street, Sturgeon Bay, Wisconsin 54235, or phone 414-743-6586.

Safari Campgrounds

Safari Campgrounds is the nation's second largest franchised campground chain with 120 campgrounds in thirty states and Canada. The campgrounds vary in size from 33 sites to over 600, with the average about 150 sites. Safaris average 70 acres in size but range from 7 acres to 2,000 acres in size. Safari permits no more than 20 camping sites to an acre, so each campsite is at least 2,000 square feet.

Safari stresses planned activities for camping families. Common are such activities as hayrides, movies, Sunday morning pancake breakfasts, bingo, square dances, campfires, volleyball, and horseshoe tournaments. All campgrounds include miniature golf, waterslides, tennis courts, kennels, grills, dock and boat rentals, game rooms, horseback riding, and fishing ponds.

A Safari franchise costs $12,000, of which $4,000 is payable at the outset and the remaining $8,000 when construction begins. The franchisee pays a royalty and service fee of 7 percent of the first $100,000 collected in site rentals and 3½ percent thereafter. The company has testimonials from franchisees showing that return on invested capital of selected franchises rose from 9 percent in the first year to 85 percent in the third year on an initial capital investment of $70,000. Campground costs are estimated at $1,200 to $1,800 per campsite, if physical characteristics are normal. The company notes that you benefit from an investment tax credit of 10 percent of qualified improvements as an offset against federal income taxes.

For further information, contact William Ellison, Franchise Director, United Safari International, Inc., Drawer 203, Knoxville, Tennessee 37919, or phone 615-584-8536.

Instant Printing

Instant printing might be the most recession-proof franchise ever devised. During the two most recent economic downturns, the industry continued to flourish. This is largely attributed to the fact that during hard times most small businesses and organizations who advertise cut back on expensive media, using instead direct-mail brochures, circulars, price lists, announcements, and other materials that are hand deliverable.

In 1976, over $7 billion was spent for printed materials in the United States. While-U-Wait printing constitutes an ever increasing percentage of this impressive figure. Why? Simple. The printed word continues to be the backbone of business communications in this nation. Many businesses realize their literature reflects directly on their reputation.

Like their counterparts in the more conventional lines of franchising, the franchisors in the printing and copying field have ingeniously developed new business opportunities. Much of this success can be ascribed to the quick print company's ability to profit from orders from large and small organizations such as parent-teachers associations, fraternal organizations, churches, and social and civic groups. Many of these groups place orders that are too small to be profitable for conventional or commercial printers. In other words, the quick-print franchisors, like many others before them, found a need and proceeded to fill it admirably. Dollars to doughnuts, they will continue to do so for the foreseeable future.

Postal Instant Press

Since the adoption of the franchise method by Bill LeVine, president of Postal Instant Press of Los Angeles, California, the firm has grown from 4 operations in 1968 to more than 365 at present. The company, which has public stockholders, boosted its net income from $49,000 in 1970 to $794,000 in 1977.

Postal Instant Press (PIP) uses a lithographic offset printing method that produces printed copies by a photo-direct method utilizing the Itek Corp. camera and A. B. Dick press. From 10 to 10,000 copies can be made in a few minutes. Of present company franchisees, some 98 percent had no previous experience. Many franchisees have opened additional PIP locations—some operate as many as six. There are presently about fifty-four PIP franchises with two or more locations.

Postal Instant Press has established an Advisory Committee of nine franchisees. Most of the members are elected by their peers. Training is offered at PIP's Los Angeles headquarters. Regional seminars are held periodically. Total estimated cost of a PIP franchise is $45,000 plus $10,000 in working capital. This includes $22,500 as a franchise fee. The cash required is $25,000, with the balance financeable. Further information may be obtained by contacting Larry Cummings, Franchise Director, Postal Instant Press, 10835 Santa Monica Boulevard, Los Angeles, California 90025, or by calling 213-475-0751.

Sir Speedy

Sir Speedy, Inc., Newport Beach, California, started in 1968 and has grown rapidly. The company is believed to rank second to Postal Instant Press in size. Its quick-printing franchises are national in scope.

Sir Speedy is the only major franchisor of quick-printing centers that offers its franchisees a cash rebate on royalties paid, based on attaining certain sales volumes. A franchisee may reduce his royalty payments from 5 percent to 0 percent on gross sales in excess of a dollar volume in any given quarterly period. As a result, for example, a center doing $23,500 per month would, under the current rebate schedule, effectively pay a royalty of 3½ percent on monthly volume.

The franchise fee is $45,000, including a $10,000 down payment, which constitutes a franchise fee. It also includes $11,000 (up to $5,000 of which may be financed by Sir Speedy) for other services, initial inventory, furniture and fixtures required. An additional $24,000 is required for equipment and fixtures. As stated, a royalty fee of 5 percent of gross sales is payable weekly. Ten-day training is provided for two persons at the company's national headquarters. For further information write Leslie Rohm, National Franchise Sales Director, Sir Speedy, Inc., P.O. Box 1790, 892 West Sixteenth Street, Newport Beach, California 92663, or call 714-642-9470.

Minuteman Press

Minuteman Press International Inc., Farmingdale, New York, is the newest franchisor of quick printing. However, the company has expanded much more rapidly than associates such as giant Minnesota Mining and Manufacturing anticipated. Minuteman currently has over 150 company-owned shops or franchises open throughout the United States. They also have over forty persons on the waiting list (waiting for suitable locations to be found, or for leases, or for training or remodeling to be completed).

Minuteman Press considers their shops to be full-service printing centers because the equipment utilized enables them to turn out top-quality multicolor jobs as easily as black and white or single-color jobs. Offset presses are supplied by Addressograph-Multigraph, while the camera is supplied by Minnesota Mining. The latter finances up to two-thirds of the entire franchise package.

Minuteman Press teaches every franchisee to use every piece of equipment, including a folding machine, plate maker, cutter, camera, and all printing presses. The franchisee receives two weeks of on-the-job training at the firm's school in Farmingdale, New York. This is followed by continued assistance and guidance in the field. Investment runs between $46,000 and $53,000, depending upon the equipment included. For further information write Roy Titus, President, Minuteman Press International Inc., 1640 New Highway, Farmingdale, New York 11735, or call 516-249-1370.

Real Estate

It is difficult to conjure a more fragmented industry than real estate. There are hundreds of thousands of small, one-man real estate brokerage firms around the country. There are real estate offices in communities much too small to ever attract other types of franchise businesses. So it is perhaps inevitable that a few aggressive franchisors would tap this big market. The result may be a big opportunity for you.

This idea really began with a somewhat older concept of real estate brokers banning together with outside national firms increasing their brokerage business through national referral services—e.g., if Mr. and Mrs. Jones move from Pennsylvania to Arizona, the Pennsylvania entity within the national network referral would, of course, refer Mr. and Mrs. Jones to an Arizona broker working under the national referral emblem.

In past years, these all-points relocation services have come and gone. The ones that stuck include Homerica, Home to Home, Inc., Inter-City Relocation Services (RELO), National Marketing Corp., and Gallery of Homes. The referral service does help a small real estate broker, and it does offer the advantage of a national logo in front of the office. The more common the logo is, the better it is for users of the limited service.

However, you should be clear on one thing—the real estate franchise is a lot more comprehensive than the simple referral service. The franchisors offer educational brochures, audio-visual aids, pooled advertising for national and regional exposure, larger advertisements, larger home photos, continuous management consultants, recruiting help, and periodic training sessions.

The market for real estate franchises is vast. One out of every five American families moves each year. Better than one of every three families moving into an area from out of town knows little or nothing of a real estate operator's local reputation. The situation is tailor made for a national franchise operation offering preinformation on families known to be transferring to the area from other parts of the nation. National exposure of listings is provided by photo listing booklets that are displayed coast to coast. Increased local exposure is created through booklet displays in local business establishments. Improved communication is afforded with lending institutions for procurement of mortgages.

Those already in the franchised real estate field hold that the broad scope of the service is pivotal. Home listing booklets from other franchisees arrive each month to be displayed in the office or reception room and can be featured in contacts with personnel directors of local businesses and industrial plants. These out-of-town booklets supplement those of the local franchisee and are themselves "listing getters." Listings, of course, are the bread-and-butter of real estate. Two-thirds of the homes purchased in the United States today are job-transfer related. This means that the transferee has little time to buy and move. Some franchisors have toll-free headquarters telephone numbers where a transferee can obtain the name of the locally franchised office where he lives and where he is moving to.

Three leading real estate franchisors are Century 21 Real Estate Corp. of Irvine, California; Red Carpet of America of Walnut Creek, California; and Realty USA of St. Louis, Missouri.

Century 21

Over the last five years, Century 21 has grown to over 2,500 franchisees in the United States and Canada. The company claims to be adding 100 new franchisees each month. Existing real estate brokers pay a franchise fee of $6,000 to Century 21, plus 6 percent of their annual gross revenues. An additional 2 percent of annual gross is put into a kitty for advertising. The parent company spends nearly $3 million annually for television advertising in sixty markets to put across its slogan,

"We're national, but we're neighborly." This exposure works, according to Art Bartlett, president of Century 21. In 1975, Century 21 franchisees sold $5.8 billion worth of homes through 145,000 separate transactions.

Century 21 has a 150-man marketing staff around the nation seeking out prospective franchisees. It sells a "master franchise" for a specific geographic territory, after which the local buyer can sell area franchises. For further information on Century 21 franchises, call William L. McQuerry, Franchise Director, at 714-752-7521, or write to company international headquarters at 18872 MacArthur Boulevard, Irvine, California 92715.

Realty USA

Realty USA is an offshoot of Interstate Referral Service, a 3,000-member real estate referral link that was established in forty-three states in 1973. New franchises cost $2,500 plus a 1½ percent annual charge based on gross commissions. The company hopes to have 5,000 offices by 1980. This, explains Tom Malone, president of Realty USA, is one-quarter of the 20,000 real estate companies in the United States who are regarded in the field as "active movers" of real estate. Over all, there are more than 200,000 real estate companies.

Realty USA is an offshoot of the Homes for Living referral service of St. Louis, founded by Mr. Malone. The company leader cites testimonials from franchisees such as one in New York state that in a short period of time went from two offices to four, increased its staff by 75 percent, and was able to increase its production goals by 50 percent for the succeeding twelve months. During this firm's first six weeks as a franchisee, one individual, who had been a million-dollar-plus producer for three years, joined the organization as an office manager and attracted ten new sales people. For further information on Realty USA call Tom Malone at this toll free number, 1-800-325-3777, or write him at 3855 Lucas and Hunt Road, St. Louis, Missouri 63121.

Red Carpet Corp. of America

Veteran California real estate man Anthony Yniguez formed Red Carpet Corp. of America in June 1966 with a network of six Red Carpet realtors, all located in Contra Costa County in northern California. The first franchises were sold for $500, compared with today's fee of $7,900. In southern California, according to the company, some of the original franchises have been resold for as much as $40,000.

Red Carpet Corp. of America prides itself on its system of strong, independent councils wherein local councils run the entire operation for their areas. Each council is made up of all Red Carpet brokers within a given marketing area. They talk over local conditions and guide their own programs in education and advertising. Mr. Yniguez says that the council provides each franchisee with more time to manage. Some 40 percent of the annual service fee is returned to the local council for use in cooperative advertising. Advertising usually accounts for between 10 and 15 percent of the average broker's gross income. Mr. Yniguez told Income Opportunities that it is not at all unusual for a Red Carpet franchisee to cover his franchise fees with income from referral sales alone. The reason for this, he says, is that the organization is coast-to-coast and has an agreement with Homerica to cover Red Carpet for referrals in Canada and parts of the United States where no local council has been established. For further information, contact Sanford L. Tullis, Vice President, at 1990 North California Boulevard, Suite 830, Walnut Creek, California 94596, or call 415-939-4550.

Rustproofing

Rustproofing is one of the most vital services provided

anywhere. It is a big and booming franchise service market, mostly because today's cars are really not prepared for the world in which they exist. With massive amounts of salt, corrosive pollutants, and moisture being faced all the time, it is little wonder that a car rusts so easily.

Left untreated, rust slowly ruins any auto—and not just its appearance. By the time rust can be seen on a car's surface, much damage has already been done. Rust starts from the inside and slowly works its way out. Salt and moisture work into inner seams and welds or onto exposed, unprotected metal deep inside the vehicle. There they combine to steadily corrode their way to the surface. After a few years, the car's structural members become seriously weakened. Tests show that cars with heavy rust damage transmit twice as much shock to the passenger compartment in a collision.

Rustproofing specialists provide a unique treatment that is generally guaranteed for five years or 50,000 miles. With more and more eyesore rusted cars on the road, motorists have come to appreciate rustproofing more and more. There are some misconceptions, however. Undercoating is basically a method of soundproofing a car rather than rustproofing it. Undercoating is mostly asphalt, which does not adhere well to metal. Undercoating cracks and comes loose in places, allowing water to become trapped underneath. Undercoating may accelerate rusting rather than prevent it.

Rustproofing is a product of the American chemical industry's genius. Its great advantage lies in the unique sealants and equally unique methods of applying rustproofing to an auto's inner surfaces—unprotected parts where moisture becomes trapped. This includes such areas as the inside of door panels and boxed-in sections of the car body, under trim strips, under headlight moldings, inside frame members, and on suspension parts and brake linings. Access holes are drilled to allow high-pressure spray tools to probe inside these hidden areas—rocker panels, fender braces, quarter panels, door seams, the hood, the trunk, and the like.

Rustproofing is one of the few industries to benefit from

inflation. As auto prices inexorably rise, motorists become more concerned with extending the life of their vehicles. Consequently, it is virtually a necessity today for a motorist to have his vehicle rustproofed. They cannot do this themselves (unlike some other auto-service functions) and so must turn to a reputable dealer. This is how the well-organized franchisors, with their thoroughly trained dealers, offer quick and effective services.

The effectiveness of rustproofing is shown by what one would have to do without it. To properly repair rust damage, a body shop would have to replace whole body panels and sections. Also, the weakened frame members underneath would have to be shored up. Such major expense could have been eliminated entirely if the car had been rustproofed early on.

Some rustproof franchisors offer a written guarantee that states that all critical areas of the motorist's car will not rust through from the inside out. A strict guarantee form is provided. If any rust does form from the inside out, the franchisor stands ready to refund the full purchase price.

Tuff-Kote Dinol

Tuff-Kote Dinol, Inc., is the outgrowth of a joint venture between Astra-Dinol of Sweden and Tuff-Kote, a well-known American supplier of corrosion-resistant chemicals, sound deadeners, sealants, and adhesives to the auto industry. Astra-Dinol had developed an exclusive penetrant, and Tuff-Kote had an exclusive aluminized sealant. The two companies joined hands in 1972 to form Tuff-Kote Dinol in Warren, Michigan. The company's process had proven to be so effective that it is guaranteed for five years, with unlimited mileage on new cars and for two years on used cars.

Today, Tuff-Kote calls itself the largest rustproofing company in the world. With operations in over forty countries, the company and its franchisees have successfully rustproofed over 6.5 million vehicles. About 3,600 licensed dealers are in operation. Fleets of commercial vehicles along with federal, state, and city governments are customers.

Tuff-Kote Dinol franchises range from $25,000 to $45,000, depending upon the market. For the lowest cost franchise, the total includes $15,000 for equipment, signs, tools, license fees, training, and protected territory. In addition, $10,000 is needed to defray rents, deposits for utilities, security deposit, insurance, advertising, and a general reserve fund.

Company officials stress that a Tuff-Kote Dinol franchise is a cash business, so accounts receivable are very small. Experience shows that most franchises become profitable in the fourth month. Management claims 30 percent profit for every car rustproofed. Yearly net profits of $25,000 to $55,000 are considered common. One-week professional training is provided for each new franchise. For further information, contact Mr. Greg Maczik, Director of Franchising, Tuff-Kote Dinol, Inc., 13650 East Ten Mile Road, Warren, Michigan 48089, or call 313-776-5000.

Endrust

Endrust Corporation, Pittsburgh, Pennsylvania, started in 1969 and has several dozen franchises in the following states: Pennsylvania, Ohio, West Virginia, Florida, Tennessee, Wisconsin, New York, Maryland, and Massachusetts. Complete national coverage in humid, coastal, and heavy-winter states is under way.

Endrust believes that it has a very competitive warranty. New, clean cars may be guaranteed for six years, with annual inspection provided for. Used cars must be rustproofed within two years or 24,000 miles, whichever occurs first. Vehicles with over 24,000 miles, over two years, may be warrantied for one year. New parts must be rustproofed within four months or 6,000 miles, whichever comes first.

Endrust claims excellent profit potential for its franchised dealers. The material cost, at current prices, is about $16 per car when Endrust is properly applied. The company says two gallons of material is adequate because it is impossible to apply more than five millimeters thickness of material without "slumping." The suggested average retail price of $85 to $110 per car shows an estimated net profit of $54.62 to $79.62 per car. Typical dealer earnings are from $14,000 to $28,000 per year.

Endrust franchisees invest $5,000 in a package that includes an airless coating unit and various accessories, including wands, eighty gallons of rustproofing material, warranty forms, mileage stickers, and bumper stickers. No franchisee is accepted unless the applicant agrees to take the free training course at the company's training depot in Cleveland, Ohio. All expenses except travel are paid by Endrust. For further information, contact Mr. S. Harrison, Endrust Corp., 401 Shady Avenue, Pittsburgh, Pennsylvania 15206.

Water Treatment

Water is everywhere, but when you drink it it may taste awful. About 85 percent of the homes in the United States have water problems involving hardness, iron, acidity, bad taste, or odors. The answer is a water softening unit that can be either sold or rented to both home and industrial users. The industry is growing at better than 20 percent per year, and franchised dealers are reportedly turning 30 percent pretax profits.

Millions and millions of gallons of soft water are required by industry for such uses as office buildings, hospitals, hotels, schools, laundries, car washes, nursing homes, restaurants, motels, apartments, trailer courts, resorts, clinics, factories, and dairies. Hard water produces a rocklike scale that builds up in pipes, dishwashing machines, water heaters, ice machines, and other appliances. Industry sources say that one-eighth inch of hard water scale on heating surfaces increases fuel consumption by 33 percent. Moreover, hard water residuals in linen, towels, and clothes reduce their service life by 15 percent to 30 percent.

In the home, soft water makes bathroom cleaning much easier and makes dishwashing almost a fun chore. Savings result during clothes washing, since much less soap and detergent is required. Water softening equipment is a young industry for young people. Industry market studies indicate that 85 percent of homeowners not having a softener would like to own one. Also, over 43 percent of nonowners wanting a softener are under thirty-five years of age.

The water conditioning franchisee is both a sales and service representative. Franchisees are trained to inspect and test home water, using efficient portable laboratories. Testing in the home is necessary because it is the only reliable way to assure proper treatment of water problems. Taste and odd odors can dissipate, and minerals can oxidize after being exposed to air. The trained franchisee can also identify problems such as rust or acid etching of chrome pipes and other metals. If hard water problems are too acute to be solved locally, franchisors in the field operate extensive water testing laboratories at their home offices.

There are many ways to make money in water conditioning. First, there is outright sale of water conditioning appliances, where markups can run more than twice the wholesale cost to you. Average wholesale cost is around $250 per unit. On this, the franchise can realize a net profit of nearly 25 percent. There is also a big business in rentals. It is estimated that 44 percent of all units manufactured are rented instead of sold. Rentals cost from $8.50 to $10.00 per month, producing an estimated pretax profit of 30 percent for the franchisee. Rental units are usually offered with a purchase option; however, industry records indicate that less than 25 percent of the rental customers elect to purchase the conditioner.

A third way to make money being a water conditioning franchisee is by salt delivery. Salt is as necessary to the performance of the conditioner as gas is to the auto, says

William M. Granger, president of WaterCare Corp., a leading franchisor. Salt costs the dealer about $1.80 for an eighty-pound bag, but this again is marked up more than twice to over $4.00 per bag. The average water conditioner uses about $80 worth of salt annually. Special soft water soaps and cleaning aids add to profitability as well.

Lindsay Company

Lindsay Company is a subsidiary of Ecodyne Corp., St. Paul, Minnesota, one of the largest companies in the world devoted to water treatment. Ecodyne has annual revenues exceeding $200 million. Lindsay, which has more than thirty years of experience manufacturing and selling water softeners, operates a five-acre production and research complex. Lindsay softeners have won the Good Housekeeping Seal of Approval and the coveted Gold Seal from the Water Conditioning Foundation.

Lindsay franchisees receive products that are backed by liberal warranties including lifetime limited warranties on mineral and brine tanks and a five-year limited warranty on brass valves. Lindsay has over 500 franchisees in the United States and has been in business since 1945. A minimum of $10,000 equity capital is required. Various credit arrangements are available to qualified applicants for equipment purchases. There is also a company-financed rental program available. Training is provided in all phases of a dealer's business, both at headquarters and in the field. For further information contact Donald D. Johnson, Dealer Development Manager, Lindsay Division, Ecodyne Corp., 455 Woodlane Drive, St. Paul, Minnesota 55119, or call 612-739-5330.

WaterCare

WaterCare Corporation, Manitowoc, Wisconsin, has been in business since 1948 and now has about 125 franchised dealers located mostly in the area from Texas and the Dakotas east to the Atlantic Ocean, and from the Canadian border to the Gulf of Mexico. The company offers its dealers a wide range of equipment and supplies.

WaterCare offers a ten-year franchise with the cost based on the experience of the individual. If the individual is an established dealer, the fee is $500. If he is new to the industry, the franchise fee is $1,500. The difference is due to the amount of training given to the dealer. A new dealer spends four days in Manitowoc and then, in his home territory, the district territory counsellor spends seven to ten days with him. Manuals and sales material are provided. These cost between $150 and $300.

The company also offers a twelve-month agreement under which the franchisee pays WaterCare one-half of the franchise fee. If at the end of twelve months he is satisfied with his franchise, he will pay the remaining one-half. If not, then the one-half fee is refunded. For further information contact William M. Granger, President, WaterCare Corp., 1520 North 24th Street, Manitowoc, Wisconsin 54220, or call 414-682-6823.

Culligan

Culligan International is the world's leading maker of household water conditioning appliances. The company was founded in Northbrook, Illinois, in 1936, and its first franchised dealership, established in Wheaton, Illinois, in 1937, is still a highly successful business and still operates under its original management. There are now 1,000 dealers in the United States and Canada.

A new Culligan dealer receives four weeks of direct training, starting with one week at International Headquarters in Northbrook, Illinois. He then spends one week with an established dealer, a week of sales training in the field, and then a week of technical service seminars, which are conducted at convenient locations around the United States. The company has stressed close cooperation with builders. This enables local dealers to sell Culligan water conditioning equipment at the time of the house sale.

Equity capital need is $20,000 or more, but the company has various credit arrangements available for the purchase of equipment from the franchisor. For further information contact Herb Hamblet, Manager - Market Development, Culligan USA, Northbrook, Illinois 60062, or call 312-498-2000.

Weight Control

There is a growing awareness on the part of the public about the dangers of being overweight. Such awareness can easily be documented. A 1977 government survey indicates that three out of every five households queried had already changed their eating programs due to a health-related diet. There are believed to be 80 million obese Americans at present.

The weight-control field has grown so rapidly that in 1977 a very successful "Diet Expo" was held in New York City with over 200 exhibitors displaying hundreds of new diet and health foods, beverages, and natural cosmetics. This is a clear sign that weight control has been accepted. Indeed, many meetings held by franchisors of weight-control programs are held in local churches or public buildings. What other kind of franchise has that much public stamp of approval?

At Diet Expo, there was graphic evidence of the success of weight-control programs. One "exhibit" was a 51-year-old Long Islander who allowed himself to balloon from 185 pounds to 410 pounds over a twenty-year period. In 1970 he joined a franchised weight-control program. Some eighteen months later, he was back down to 190 pounds, and he has maintained this level ever since. This individual loved the Diet Control Center program so much that he is now a franchisee in Nassau County, New York.

A major improvement on the part of the weight-control franchisors is the diet itself. There is nothing new about unpalatable, bland diets. What is new is that leading franchisors include ethnic or exotic foods in their weight-loss plans. Some offer three full meals per day plus snacks from a wide selection and variety of foods. Fish and liver are not required. Such oddities as cheeseburgers, desserts, wines, and liquors are included in some dining schedules.

Weight-control franchises are relatively low cost. Some are available for only $5,000. This usually includes supplies to put you in business, including confidential operating manuals, a complete bookkeeping system, intensive training sessions, and area visits. Well-established franchises benefit by medical referrals and interest on the part of members of organizations where meetings are held.

Diet Workshop

Diet Workshop Inc., East Meadow, New York, is a nationally franchised organization with over 1,400 groups meeting weekly throughout the United States, Canada, and Bermuda. The company was founded in 1965 by Lois Lindauer, who began by teaching a group of Boston women about the role of nutrition in losing weight. A nutrition consultant, Dr. Morton B. Glenn, has been affiliated with Diet Workshop since 1968.

Diet Workshop has over seventy franchises in operation at the present time. President Lindauer says that 45 percent of available franchise areas are operating. Unique promotions are offered, and local media are readily supplied with promotional material on weight loss. Typical of company promotions, during a nationwide Lose-A-Thon, Diet Workshop raised $65,000 for CARE recently.

Diet Workshop says it is the first weight-control franchise to introduce the techniques of behavior modification to group weight control. By focusing on eating-behavior problems as well as food problems, Diet Workshop members learn to exchange old, bad eating habits as they learn about proper foods. Area franchises cost $5,000. For further information, write Lois L. Lindauer, International Director, The Diet Workshop, Inc., 111 Washington St., Brookline, MA 02146, or call 617-739-2222.

Diet Control Centers

Diet Control Centers, Inc., Union, New Jersey, is one of the fastest growing weight reduction business organizations in the United States. Founded in 1968 by three New Jersey house-wives, the company now has about thirty franchises. Modeled after Weight Watchers, Diet Control Centers' method of teaching weight loss strongly emphasizes controlled portions of commonly eaten foods, a series of exercises, and a comprehensive program of behavior modification.

Classes, averaging forty members per class weekly, are held in public meeting rooms and schools. Members pay a registration fee of $7.00 and a weekly fee of $3.00. The program, including many recipes, is available to the general public nationally in a book published by Bantam in 1976 entitled *Slim Forever: The Diet Control Centers Diet.* A company newspaper is published six times per year and distributed throughout the entire membership as well as in such outlets as supermarkets and restaurants.

The company offers franchises starting at $5,000, which includes supplies, training, supervision, and bookkeeping. Diet Control Centers projects an annual gross profit of from $13,260 to $51,324 deriving from four to sixteen two-hour weekly meetings, with thirty persons attending each meeting. Income is derived from weekly dues, new registration fees, and the sale of scales and cookbooks. Total weekly revenues run from $458 to $1,832. Weekly expenses include franchise royalties (15 percent), meeting rentals, cost of scales and cookbooks, and advertising. Total weekly expenses run from $203 to $845, leaving total weekly gross profits of from $255 to $987. For further information write to Ruth Landesberg, Executive Vice

President, Diet Control Centers, Inc., 1021 Stuyvesant Avenue, Union, New Jersey, or call 201-687-0007.

Weight Place

The Weight Place is a new program for weight reduction and weight maintenance offered by Fat Fighters, Inc. of Los Altos, California. There are three main parts to the Weight Place program: a 100 percent natural-food supplement, daily counseling, and nutritionally balanced and chemically controlled diet plans that are tailored to the body needs of each individual client. The proprietary food supplement is an invert sugar with special B-complex vitamins and protein, in an isolate carrier, which are absorbed directly into the bloodstream through the stomach wall without having to pass through the entire digestive tract as sucrose in order to be utilized by the body. This process reduces the hunger factor, provides an instantaneous and prolonged energy lift, and brings the blood sugar to a normal level.

The food supplement is given out daily by the franchised counselor, thus requiring the client to visit the center so that the counselor has the opportunity to weigh, counsel, and encourage, and to check the client's daily progress. The cost includes the daily food supplement, the nutritionally balanced and chemically controlled diet plans, recipe booklets, and daily counseling. A two-week program costs $49, or $3.50 per day. A six-week program costs $126, or $3.00 per day. For those on the program, weight is being lost at an average of one-half to three-quarters of a pound per day for women, and three-quarters to one pound per day for men. This translates to seven to fourteen pounds in a two-week program or twenty-one to forty-two pounds in a six-week program.

Since its inception, over 250 Weight Place operations, primarily in California, have begun. New units are being opened at the rate of five to ten per month. The initial franchise fee is $8,000, and royalty and service fees are 6 percent of minimum gross receipts from program sales. The franchisee obtains nutrients, training, program literature, office equipment, and other assistance. A training program, totaling 361 hours, is given at the Weight Place center in Los Altos, California. For further information contact Nina J. Kiger, President, Fat Fighters, Inc., 4546 El Camino Real, Suite O, Los Altos, California 94002.

14

Directory of Franchises

The following pages represent a comprehensive roster of leading established franchisors with complete addresses, phone numbers, and the name of the franchise director or key official to whom inquiries about further information should be directed. Each one of the several hundred listings shown below represents the current membership of the International Franchise Association, Washington, D.C., the industry's leading trade organization. IFA members are accepted into the association only after meeting stringent requirements, which involve number of franchises, length of time in business, and financial stability. All applicants for membership are investigated extensively by IFA's Executive Committee. While the author implies no guarantee of success in any of these franchises, it is probably the most reputable list of franchisors in existence today.

AAMCO TRANSMISSIONS, INC.
Transmission service centers
408 East Fourth Street
Bridgeport, Pennsylvania
    19405
215-277-4000
    Franchise Director: Ronald
        Smythe, Vice President

A & W INTERNATIONAL, INC.
Fast-food restaurants
922 Broadway
P. O. Box 1039
Santa Monica, California
    90406
213-395-3261
    Franchise Director: John F.
        Osterman, Director
        Franchise Administra-
        tion

ABC MOBILE SYSTEMS
Mobile brake repair service
9420 Telstar Avenue, Suite 101
El Monte, California 91731
213-579-7260
    Franchise Director: Ronald
        Norris, Executive Vice
        President

ADIA SERVICES, INC.
Temporary help service
P. O. Box 2768
64 Willow Place

Menlo Park, California 94025
415-324-0696
   Brian G. Dailey, Vice
      President and
      Franchise Director

ARBY'S, INC., d.b.a. ARBY'S
   INTERNATIONAL
Fast-food restaurants
   specializing in roast beef
   sandwiches
4944 Belmont Avenue
Youngstown, Ohio 44512
216-759-9400
   Franchise Director: Joseph
      G. Smaltz, Vice
      President, Licensing

ARTHUR MURRAY, INC.
Ballroom dancing
1077 Ponce de Leon
   Boulevard
Coral Gables, Florida 33134
305-445-9645
   Neil Evans, Assistant Vice
      President, Franchising

ARTHUR TREACHER'S
   FISH & CHIPS, INC.
Specialty restaurant chain
1328 Dublin Road
Columbus, Ohio 43215
614-486-3636
   Edward Lifman, President

A-TECH, INC.
*Nondestructive roof moisture
    survey*
2631 North Meade Street
P.O. Box 1954
Appleton, Wisconsin 54.~'3
414-733-7324
    Richard G. Anderson,
        President

AVIS RENT A CAR
    SYSTEM, INC.
*Renting and leasing of motor
    vehicles*
1701 K Street, NW, Suite 1001
Washington, D.C. 20006
202-296-0443
    Franchise Director: Robert
        McDowell

BARBIZON
    INTERNATIONAL,
    INC.
*Modeling, personal
    improvement, and
    fashion schools*
689 Fifth Avenue
New York, New York 10022
212-355-5700
    Franchise Director: Barry B.
        Wolff, Executive Vice
        President

THE BECKER MILK CO.
   LTD.
Convenience stores
671 Warden Avenue
Scarborough, Ontario
Canada, M1L 3Z7
416-698-2591
   Raj Dargan, Director of
   Franchising

BIG BOY RESTAURANTS
   OF AMERICA
Family restaurants
1001 East Colorado Street
Glendale, California 91209
213-241-3161
   R. Raskin, Director of
   Franchising

BIG RED Q QUICKPRINT
   CENTERS
Instant printing and copying
3131 Douglas Road
Toledo, Ohio 43606
419-473-1551
   Franchise Director: Pete
   Bozzo

BIG TOP DELI CORP.
Deli-style sandwich shops
444 Seabreeze Boulevard,
   Suite 710
Daytona Beach, Florida 32018
904-258-5417
   Franchise Director: Jon
   Elliott

BONANZA
    INTERNATIONAL,
    INC.
Fast-food-steak house chain
1000 Campbell Centre
8350 North Central
    Expressway
Dallas, Texas 75206
214-363-1011
    Edward F. Kosan, Director
        of Franchise Services

BOSTON PIZZA &
    SPAGHETTI HOUSE,
    LTD.
Fast-food restaurants
14504 125th Avenue
Edmonton, Alberta
Canada T5L 3C5
403-452-1690
    Franchise Director: R. Ian
        Barrigan, General
        Manager and Treasurer

BRESLER'S 33 FLAVORS,
    INC.
*Bresler's 33 Flavors Ice Cream
    Shops*
4010 Belden Avenue
Chicago, Illinois 60639
312-227-6700
    Stanley Bresler, Chairman
        of the Board

BROWN'S CHICKEN
*Chicken carry-out and dine-in
    restaurants*
800 Enterprise Drive
Oak Brook, Illinois 60521
312-654-0730
    Frank Portillo, President

BROWN DERBY, INC.
Restaurants
7850 Northfield Road
Cleveland, Ohio 44146
216-439-6400
    Franchise Director: Bernard
        C. Johnson, Secretary

BUBBLE UP COMPANY,
    INC.
Franchisor of Bubble Up
2800 North Talman Avenue
Chicago, Illinois 60618
312-463-4600
    Franchise Director: Roy
        Gurvey, Executive Vice
        President

BUDGET RENT A CAR
    CORP.
*International franchisor of
    Budget Rent a Car
    operations*
35 East Wacker Drive
Chicago, Illinois 60601
312-641-0424
    Clifton E. Haley, Sr. Vice
        President, Franchise
        Sales

BURGER CHEF SYSTEMS, INC.
Fast-food restaurants
3500 DePauw Boulevard,
    Blvd. #2
P.O. Box 927
Indianapolis, Indiana 46206
317-299-8400
  Roger A. Schafer, Vice
    President, Franchise
    Operations

BURGER KING CORP.
Fast-food restaurants
P.O. Box 520783, Biscayne
    Annex
Miami, Florida 33152
305-596-7011
  Jeff Seeberger, Director,
    Franchise Development

BURGER QUEEN ENTERPRISES
Fast-food restaurants
4000 Dupont Circle
P.O. Box 6014
Louisville, Kentucky 40206
502-897-1766
  Chief Executive and
    Franchise Director:
    George E. Clark,
    President

CASSANO ENTERPRISES,
INC.
Fast-food restaurants
1700 East Stroop Road
Dayton, Ohio 45429
513-294-8400
Franchise Director: Charles
Rowse

THE CATO CORP.
*Retailer of women's fashion
apparel*
P.O. Box 2416
Charlotte, North Carolina
28234
704-554-8510
Franchise Director:
D. Michael Jordan

CENTURY 21 REAL
ESTATE CORP.
Real estate franchising
18872 McArthur Boulevard
P.O. Box 19564
Irvine, California 92713
714-752-7521
Franchise Director: William
L. McQuerry

CHARLIE CHAN FAST
FOODS, INC.
Chinese food products
50 Karago Avenue
Youngstown, Ohio 44512
216-758-0525
Richard A. D'Onofrio,
President

CHART HOUSE, INC.
Fast-food restaurants
666 Jefferson Street, Suite
   1000
Lafayette, Louisiana 70501
318-233-6400
   John Spearing, Director of
      Franchise Relations

CHICKEN DELIGHT,
   Division of Action
   Traders, Inc.
Fast-food restaurants
227 East Sunshine, Suite 119
Springfield, Missouri 65807
417-862-7875
   Franchise Director: Wendell
      E. Lejeune, Divisional
      Manager

CHURCH'S FRIED
   CHICKEN, INC.
Fried chicken restaurants
355 Spencer Lane
P.O. Box BH001
San Antonio, Texas 78284
512-735-9392
   Franchise Director: Roy D.
      Collins, Vice President,
      Licensing

THE COCA-COLA CO.
Soft drinks
310 North Avenue
P.O. Drawer 1734
Atlanta, Georgia 30301
404-897-2121
    H. A. Arnold, Vice
        President, Operating
        Mgr., Fountain Sales
        Dept.

COFFEE SYSTEM, INC.
Coffee and beverage services
    to offices
Independence Square West
Philadelphia, Pennsylvania
    19106
215-574-5470
Franchise Director: Francis X.
    McCoy, President

COMMANDER BOARD
    INTERNATIONAL,
    INC.
Manufacturer of visual
    communication products
2201 Fifty-ninth Street
St. Louis, Missouri 63110
314-644-0700
    Franchise Director: Richard
        D. Mills, Vice
        President

COMPREHENSIVE
  ACCOUNTING
  SERVICE CO.
Bookkeeping services
901 East Galena Boulevard
Aurora, Illinois 60505
312-898-1234
  Franchise Director: Daniel
    L. Mesch, Manager of
    Program Counselors

CONVENIENCE FOOD
  MART, INC.
Superette grocery stores
875 North Michigan Avenue,
  Suite 1401
Chicago, Illinois 60611
312-751-1500
  Franchise Director: William
    R. Sandberg, Executive
    Vice President

COPPER PENNY FAMILY
  COFFEE SHOPS
Restaurants
6837 Lankershim Boulevard
North Hollywood, California
  91605
213-982-2620
  Franchise Director: Richard
    Sandnes

COTTMAN
TRANSMISSION
SYSTEMS, INC.
*Automobile transmission
repair centers*
575 Virginia Drive
Fort Washington,
Pennsylvania 19034
215-643-5885
Franchise Director: Jerome
Marcus, Executive Vice
President

CRAIG FOOD
INDUSTRIES, INC.
*Mexican fast-food restaurant
chain*
3745 South 250 West
P.O. Box 9255
Ogden, Utah 84409
801-621-5464
Franchise Director: Brent
Buckner

DAD'S ROOT BEER CO.
Franchisor of Dad's Root Beer
2800 North Talman Avenue
Chicago, Illinois 60618
312-463-4600
Franchise Director: Roy
Gurvey, Executive Vice
President

DAIHO SANGYO CO., LTD.
Home, auto retail stores
1-12, Oyodo Minami
1-chome, Oyodo-Ku
Osaka, Japan 531
   Chief Executive: Toshio
      Sumino, President

DAYS INNS OF AMERICA,
   INC.
Motels, inns, and lodges
2751 Buford Highway, NE
Atlanta, Georgia 30324
404-325-4000
   Franchise Director: James
      D. Landon, Senior Vice
      President

DER WIENERSCHNITZEL
   INTERNATIONAL,
   INC.
Fast-food restaurants
4440 Von Karman
Newport Beach, California
   92660
714-752-6511
   L. J. Clemensen, Director of
      Franchise Operations

THE DIET WORKSHOP,
   INC.
Group weight control
111 Washington Street
Brookline, Massachusetts
   02146
617-739-2222
   Lois Lindauer, President

DINO'S, INC.
Pizza restaurants
2085 Inkster Road
P.O. Box 505
Garden City, Michigan 48135
313-261-9460
    Franchise Director: Bill
        Wischman, Director of
        Finance

DOCTOR'S ASSOCIATES,
    INC.
Fast-food sandwich shops
25 High Street
Milford, Connecticut 06460
203-877-4281
    Franchise Director: Richard
        T. Pilchen

DOG'N SUDS, INC.
Fast-food restaurant chain
1420-32 Crestmont Avenue
Camden, New Jersey 08103
609-966-7500
    Franchise Director: Michael
        Fessler, Executive Vice
        President

DOMESTICARE, INC.
Residential cleaning service
190 Godwin Avenue
Midland Park, New Jersey
    07432
201-447-3737
    Franchise Director: William
        A. Jasper

DOMINO'S PIZZA, INC.
Pizza making and delivery
2865 Boardwalk Drive
Ann Arbor, Michigan 48104
313-668-4000
Franchise Director: Oscar
Schreiber

DRIVE LINE SERVICE,
INC.
*Drive shaft repair and service
shops*
704 Houston Street
P.O. Box 782
West Sacramento, California
95691
916-371-8117
Chief Executive: Louis D.
Wilson, President

DUNHILL PERSONNEL
SYSTEM, INC.
Employment agencies
1 Old Country Road
Carle Place, New York 11514
516-741-5400
Edward Kushell, President,
Los Angeles, California

DUNKIN' DONUTS OF
AMERICA, INC.
Coffee and donut shops
P.O. Box 317
Randolph, Massachusetts
02368
617-961-4000
Franchise Directors: Al
Vermiere, Herb Rust,
David Smith, Lee
Bourdon

DURACLEAN
INTERNATIONAL
*Carpet and furniture cleaning
franchise*
2151 Waukegan Road
Deerfield, Illinois 60015
312-945-2000
Chief Executive: Ford A.
Marsh, President

DUSKIN COMPANY, LTD.
*Manufacturing, renting,
cleaning equipment.*
*Fast food: Mister Donut
Division*
Sekaicho Building
6-24 Nakatsu 1-chome
Oyodo-Ku
Osaka, Japan 531
Franchise Director:
Shigeharu Komai,
Executive Vice
President

ECONO-TRAVEL MOTOR
HOTEL CORP.
*Econo-Travel Motor Hotels
and Econo-Lodges*
#20 Koger Executive Center,
Suite 100
P.O. Box 12188
Norfolk, Virginia 23502
804-461-6111
Franchise Director: I. T.
Van Patten III, Director
of Development

ELAINE POWERS FIGURE SALONS, INC.
Owners, operators, and franchisor of ladies figure salons
105 West Michigan Street
Milwaukee, Wisconsin 53220
414-273-2200
Franchise Director:
Elizabeth Browning

ELECTRONIC REALTY ASSOCIATES, INC.
Real estate brokerage firms
4900 College Boulevard
Shawnee Mission, Kansas 66211
913-341-8400
Chief Executive: James A. Jackson, President

ENGINEERING CORP. OF AMERICA
Engineering job shop
2460 Garden Road
Monterey, California 93940
408-649-3590
Franchise Director: Vernon W. Haas, President

EVERFAST, INC.
Retail fabric trade
Rockford Road, Bancroft Mills
P.O. Box 670
Wilmington, Delaware 19899
302-652-3671
Franchise Director: Bert G. Kerstetter, President

E-Z KEEP SYSTEMS
*Financial management and
    counseling*
5324 Ekwill Street
Santa Barbara, California
    93111
805-964-4768
    Franchise Director: W. O.
        Kringle

FAMOUS RECIPE FRIED
    CHICKEN, INC.
Fast-food (chicken) franchisor
11315 Reed Hartman
    Highway, Suite 200
Cincinnati, Ohio 45241
513-984-4000
    Franchise Director: Robert
        D. Acker, Director of
        Franchise Sales

FARREL'S ICE CREAM
    PARLOUR
    RESTAURANTS
Ice cream parlors
5161 River Road
Washington, D. C. 20016
301-986-7085
    Franchise Director: Richard
        Ramsburg

FLOWER WORLD OF
    AMERICA, INC.
Florist
1655 Imperial Way, Mid-
    Atlantic Park
P. O. Box 1655
Woodbury, New Jersey 08096
609-845-2426
    Franchise Director: Robert
        Sheets, President

FLOWERAMA OF AMERICA, INC.
Franchise floral shop operation
3165 West Airline Highway
Waterloo, Iowa 50701
319-291-6004
Franchise Director: Bryan Patzkowski

FRANCHISE GROWTH CORP.
Snack foods
101 Thirty-first Avenue, Box No. 1058
Rock Island, Illinois 61201
309-788-8416
Franchise Director: Roger R. Glen, Vice President, Sales

FROSTIE ENTERPRISES
Soft drink bottling
1420 Crestmont Avenue
Camden, New Jersey 08103
609-966-7500
Franchise Director: Michael W. Fessler, Vice President

GALLERY OF HOMES, INC.
Residential real estate broker franchisor
1001 International Boulevard
Atlanta, Georgia 30354
800-241-8320
Henry F. Carter, President

GENERAL BUSINESS
SERVICES, INC.
*Small business counseling
and tax service*
51 Monroe Street
Rockville, Maryland 20850
301-424-1040
Franchise Director: Robert
F. Turner, Vice
President, Field
Development Group

GETTING TO KNOW YOU
INTERNATIONAL
(NO. 2) LTD.
Homeowner welcome service
49 Watermill Lane
Great Neck, New York 11022
516-829-8210
Franchise Director: Richard
F. Wynn, Vice
President, Marketing

GILBERT LANE
PERSONNEL
Permanent personnel agency
750 Main Street
Hartford, Connecticut 06103
203-278-7700
Joan Castelli, Director of
Franchise Operations

GINGISS
  INTERNATIONAL,
  INC.
Men's formal wear, rental and
  sales
180 North LaSalle Street,
  Suite 1111
Chicago, Illinois 60601
312-236-2333
  Franchise Director: John
      W. Heiser, Vice
      President

GOLDEN SKILLET
  CORPORATION
Fast-food, fried chicken chain
2819 Parham Road
Richmond, Virginia 23229
804-747-0650
  Franchise Director: Michael
      G. Thompson,
      Marketing Director

GRANDMA LEE'S
  INTERNATIONAL
  HOLDINGS, LTD.
Bakery and eating outlets
3258 Wharton Way
Mississauga, Ontario
Canada L4X 2C4
416-625-5055
  Chief Executive: A. P.
      Biggs, President

GRIZZLY BEAR, INC.
Pizza Parlor Restaurants
Route 3, Box 100, Highway
    201
P.O. Box 397
Ontario, Oregon 97914
503-889-7666
    Chief Executive: Donn H.
        Mires, President

GUARANTEE CARPET
    CLEANING AND DYE
    CO.
*Franchisor—carpet cleaning
    and dye*
2953 Powers Avenue
P.O. Box 40749
Jacksonville, Florida 32203
904-733-8211
    Chief Executive: Frank
        Woodruff, President

H & R BLOCK, INC.
Tax preparation
4410 Main Street
Kansas City, Missouri 64111
816-753-6900
    Franchise Director: William
        T. Ross, Vice
        President, Director,
        Administrative
        Operations

HARDEE'S FOOD SYSTEMS, INC.
Fast-food hamburger restaurants
1233 North Church Street
P.O. Box 1619
Rocky Mount, North
    Carolina 27801
919-977-2000
    Donald R. Mucci, Director
        of Franchise
        Development

HERCULES RUSTPROOFING
Automotive rustproofing
Hercules Building
231 Hay Street
Johnstown, Pennsylvania
    15902
814-536-3737
    Franchise Director:
        Benjamin Davis

HICKORY FARMS OF OHIO, INC.
Cheese and specialty food stores
300 Holland Road
Maumee, Ohio 43537
419-893-7611
    Franchise Director: Richard
        J. Bordeaux, Executive
        Vice President

HILTON INNS, INC.
Franchise division of Hilton Hotels Corp.
9880 Wilshire Boulevard
Beverly Hills, California 90210
213-278-4321
Franchise Director: Lloyd S. Farwell, Senior Vice President

HOLIDAY INNS, INC.
Hotel/motel operations
3742 Lamar Avenue
Memphis, Tennessee 38118
901-362-4001
Franchise Director: Mickey Powell, Division Vice President

HOLIDAY INN TRAV-L-PARKS
Recreational vehicle parks for campers
3796 Lamar Avenue
Memphis, Tennessee 38118
901-362-4857
Franchise Director: Davis Smith, Division Vice President

HUDDLE HOUSE, INC.
Restaurants
2947 East Ponce de Leon
    Avenue
Decatur, Georgia 30030
404-377-8181
    Franchise Director: Charlie
        N. Crowder, Vice
        President

IHOP CORP.
Retail restaurant operations
6837 Lankershim Boulevard
North Hollywood, California
    91605
213-982-2620
    Franchise Director: Joel
        Justice, Vice President

INSTY-PRINTS, INC.
Instant printing centers
417 North Fifth Street
Minneapolis, Minnesota
    55401
612-335-9573
    Franchise Director: John O.
        Prater, Marketing
        Director

INTERNATIONAL DAIRY
    QUEEN, INC.
Fast food, soft serve
5701 Green Valley Drive
Minneapolis, Minnesota
    55435
612-830-0200
    Franchise Director: Gil
        Stemmerman, Vice
        President, Franchise
        Development

INTERNATIONAL HOUSE OF PANCAKES
Restaurant franchising
6837 Lankershim Boulevard
North Hollywood, California
    91605
213-982-2620
    Designee and Franchise
        Director: Joel R.
        Justice, Vice President,
        Franchise Relations

INTERNATIONAL MULTIFOODS CORP.
Mister Donut of America
1200 Multifoods Building
Minneapolis, Minnesota
    55402
612-340-3300
    Joe Dubanoski, Vice
        President, Mister
        Donut of America

JELLYSTONE CAMPGROUNDS, LTD.
*Franchisor of deluxe high
    amenity campgrounds
    and budget motels*
236 Michigan Street
Sturgeon Bay, Wisconsin
    54235
414-743-6586
    Franchise Director: James
        E. Webb, Vice
        President, Marketing

JERRICO, INC.
Restaurant chains
101 Jerrico Drive
P. O. Box 11988
Lexington, Kentucky 40579
606-268-5211
   Warren W. Rosenthal,
      President

JERRY'S RESTAURANTS
Restaurant chain
101 Jerrico Drive
P. O. Box 8088
Lexington, Kentucky 40579
606-268-5211
   Eugene O. Getchell, Vice
      President of
      Franchising

JUICY LUCY
Fresh fruit juice/snack bar
   operations
P. O. Box 8686
Joahnnesburg 2000
Republic of South Africa
   Chief Executive: Barry N.
      Aitken, President

KEN'S PIZZA PARLORS,
   INC.
Pizza parlors
4441 South Seventy-second
   East Avenue
Tulsa, Oklahoma 74145
918-663-8880
   Franchise Director: Michael
      E. Bartlett, Vice President,
      and Secretary

KFC CORP.
*Franchisor of Kentucky Fried
    Chicken and Zantigo
    Mexican-American
    restaurants*
1441 Gardiner Lane
P.O. Box 32070
Louisville, Kentucky 40232
502-459-8600
    John F. Cox, Vice
        President, Franchising
        and Public Affairs

**KINGS ROW SYSTEMS,
    INC.**
*Fireplaces, fireplace
    accessories, and
    equipment*
P.O. Box 28126
Columbus, Ohio 43228
614-878-9331
    Franchise Director: William
        C. Benson, Vice
        President

**KARMELKORN SHOPPES,
    INC.**
*Popcorn confections and
    related snacks*
101 Thirty-first Avenue
Rock Island, Illinois 61201
309-788-8416
    Franchise Director: Roger
        R. Glen, Vice President

KNAPP SHOE CO.
Manufacture and sale of shoes
One Knapp Centre
Brockton, Massachusetts
    02401
617-588-9000
    Franchise Director: Walter
        E. Cullen, Manager,
        Franchise Division

KWIK-KOPY CORP.
Instant printing
5225 Hollister Road
Houston, Texas 77040
713-688-2571
    Franchise Director: Henry
        S. Eason, Executive
        Vice President

**LADY MADONNA
    MANAGEMENT CORP.**
*Manufacturer of maternity
    apparel*
36 East Thirty-first Street
New York, New York 10016
212-685-4555
    Franchise Director: Ronald
        Sommers, Vice
        President

LAROSA'S, INC.
Italian pizzerias
2411 Boudinot
Cincinnati, Ohio 45238
513-451-1574
    Franchise Director: Stewart
        A. Smetts

LAWN DOCTOR, INC.
Automated lawn service
P.O. Box 186, Conover Road
Wickatunk, New Jersey 07765
201-946-9700
   Franchise Director: Pete
      Thompson

LITTLE PROFESSOR
   BOOK CENTERS, INC.
Bookstore franchising
33200 Capitol Avenue
Livonia, Michigan 48150
313-525-1500
   Franchise Director: Albert
      C. Van Roden

LONG JOHN SILVER'S,
   INC.
*Fast food seafood restaurant
   (Division of Jerrico, Inc.)*
101 Jerrico Drive
Lexington, Kentucky 40579
606-268-5211
   Eugene O. Getchell, Vice
      President of
      Franchising

LOVE'S ENTERPRISES
Fast-food restaurants
4942 Vineland Avenue
North Hollywood, California
   91601
213-877-0783
   Franchise Director: Ronald
      Mesker, Vice President

LEE MYLES ASSOCIATES CORP.
Automatic transmission repair
59-24 Maurice Avenue
New York, New York 11378
212-386-0100
Franchise Director: Allen Kern

LELLY'S DRIVE IN PHOTOS, INC.
Retail photo stores
4641 State Road 84
Ft. Lauderdale, Florida 33314
305-587-5250
Franchise Director: Kenneth H. Lelly, President

LIEN CHEMICAL CO.
Restroom sanitation service
9229 West Grand Avenue
Franklin Park, Illinois 60131
312-455-5000
Franchise Director: Rich Crane, Vice President and Secretary

LITTLE CAESAR ENTERPRISES, INC.
Pizza Parlors
38700 Grand River Avenue
Farmington Hills, Michigan 48018
313-478-6200
Charles Jones, Vice President of Franchising

LUMS RESTAURANT
   CORP.
Fast-food family restaurants
8410 N.W. 53rd Terrace, #200
Miami, Florida 33166
305-592-5867
   Charles A. Greer, Director
      of Franchising

MAACO ENTERPRISES,
   INC.
Auto painting and body
   works
381 Brooks Road
King of Prussia, Pennsylvania
   19406
215-265-6606
   Franchise Director: George
      Gardner

MAC'S CONVENIENCE
   STORES LTD.
Convenience stores
10 Commander Boulevard
Scarborough, Ontario
Canada M1S 3T2
416-291-4441
   R. S. Maich, President

MAJIK MARKET
   CONVENIENCE
   STORES
Convenience stores
(Division of Munford, Inc.)
P.O. Box 304
Conley, Georgia 30027
404-363-1440
   Franchise Director: Jim
      Cooper

MANAGEMENT
RECRUITERS
INTERNATIONAL,
INC.
Personnel placement
1015 Euclid Avenue
Cleveland, Ohio 44115
216-696-1122
Robert A. Angell, Vice
President, Director of
Franchise Marketing

MANPOWER, INC.
Temporary help service
5301 North Ironwood Road
Milwaukee, Wisconsin 53217
414-961-1000
Franchise Director: William
J. Gallagher, Vice
President, International
Franchise Affairs

MARCOIN, INC.
*Management services for
retail petroleum industry*
150 South Washington Street
Falls Church, Virginia 22046
703-683-9918
Chief Executive: Fred G.
Harris, Chairman

MARRIOTT CORP.
*Restaurants, hotels, contract
    food services, theme
    parks, in-flite catering*
5161 River Road
Bethesda, Maryland 20016
301-986-5201
    Randall L. Frazier, Vice
        President and
        Controller, Restaurant
        Operations

**MARY MOPPET'S DAY
    CARE CENTERS, INC.**
Nursery and day care schools
202 West Huntington Drive
Temple, Arizona 85282
602-967-2063
    Gerald J. Spresser,
        President

**MATCHMAKER HOME
    MARKETING
    SYSTEMS, INC.**
Real estate systems
1116 Arsenal Street
P.O. Box 281
Watertown, New York 13601
315-782-0300
    Franchise Director: Pat
        Massaro, Senior Vice
        President

McDONALD'S CORP.
Fast-food restaurants
McDonald's Plaza
Oak Brook, Illinois 60521
312-887-3200
Franchise Director: John L.
Coons, Senior Vice
President

McGRAW-EDISON CO.
*Martinizing dry cleaning
stores*
5050 Section Avenue
Cincinnati, Ohio 45212
513-731-5500
Franchise Director: Allan
Greenweller, Manager

MEDICINE SHOPPE
INTERNATIONAL,
INC.
Professional pharmacy chain
100 Progress Parkway, Suite
111
Maryland Heights, Missouri
63043
314-878-0050
Franchise Director: Gerald
Rhydderch, Vice
President, Marketing

MEINEKE DISCOUNT
MUFFLER SHOPS,
INC.
Muffler shops
6330 West Loop South, Suite
103
Bellaire, Texas 77401
713-661-0414
Franchise Director: Al
Hirsh, Director of
Franchise Sales

MIDAS-INTERNATIONAL
CORP.
Retail muffler shops
222 South Riverside Plaza
Chicago, Illinois 60606
312-648-5600
Franchise Director: William
R. Strahan, Vice
President, Franchise
Operations

MIGHTY DISTRIBUTING
SYSTEM OF AMERICA,
INC.
*Auto parts to after-market
service stations*
7146 Montevideo Road
Jessup, Maryland 20794
301-799-2188
Chief Executive: Dallas F.
Wallace, President

MISTER DONUT OF AMERICA, INC.
Franchising donut shops
1200 Multifoods Building
Minneapolis, Minnesota
    55402
612-340-3300
    Franchise Director: Ken
        Kuhn, Vice President
        of Development

MISTER SOFTEE, INC.
*Franchising of mobile ice
    cream trucks*
901 East Clements Bridge
    Road
Runnemede, New Jersey
    08078
609-931-0200
    Franchise Director: James
        F. Conway, Vice
        President, General
        Manager

MOM'S HOMEMADE ICE CREAM PARLORS, INC.
Ice cream parlors
Diamond Hill, Penthouse D
2420 West Twenty-sixth
    Avenue
Denver, Colorado 80211
303-433-8501
    Franchise Director: Marty
        Clancy, Vice President

MR. HERO SANDWICH
SYSTEMS, INC.
*Fast-food and carry-out
restaurants*
6902 Pearl Road
Parma, Ohio 44130
216-842-6000
Franchise Director: Charles
Fever

MOM 'N' POP'S HAM
HOUSE, INC.
Restaurants
P.O. Box 399
Spring Street
Claremont, North Carolina
28610
704-459-7626
Franchise Director: Richard
S. Howard, Vice
President

MR. QUICK, INC.
Fast-food restaurants
3760 Forty-first Street
P.O. Box 190
Moline, Illinois 61265
309-762-7301
Franchise Director: Lee A.
Womack, President

MR. STEAK, INC.
Family steak houses
5100 Race Court
Denver, Colorado 80217
303-292-3070
Dale D. Thompson, Vice
President of Franchise
Sales

MUNFORD, INC.
Diversified franchising
68 Brookwood Drive
Atlanta, Georgia 30357
404-873-6641
    J.S. Cooper, Jr., Director of
    Sales

MY NAILS, INC.
Manufacturer of beauty aids
5354 North High Street
Columbus, Ohio 43214
614-846-0600
    Chief Executive: Bonnie A.
        McAllister, President
        and Treasurer

MY WORKSHOP, INC.
Do-it-yourself picture framing
3308 Ella Boulevard, Suite K
Houston, Texas 77018
713-688-2571
    Franchise Director: Henry
        S. Eason, Executive
        Vice President

NATHAN'S FAMOUS, INC.
Fast-food restaurants
1515 Broadway
New York, New York 10036
212-869-0600
    Franchise Director: Harold
        Norbitz, Vice President,
        Franchising, Real
        Estate

NEW ENGLAND LOG
  HOMES, INC.
Manufacturing pre-log homes
2301 State Street
P.O. Box 5056
Hamden, Connecticut 06518
203-562-9981
  Franchise Director: Edward
    Sink, Sales Manager

NOBLE ROMAN'S, INC.
Pizza restaurants
2909 Buick-Cadillac
    Boulevard
P.O. Box 1089
Bloomington, Indiana 47401
812-339-3533
  Franchise Director: Jack M.
    Borowski

THE OLSTEN CORP.
Temporary personnel services
One Merrick Avenue
Westbury, New York 11590
516-997-7200
  Chief Executive: William
    Olsten, President
    Chairman

OMELET SHOPPE, INC.
24-hour family restaurants
129 Citation Court
Birmingham, Alabama 35209
205-942-4774
  Chief Executive: Bill B.
    Ingram, President

**OPEN PANTRY FOOD
    MART CORP.**
Convenience stores
3055 East Sixty-third Street
Cleveland, Ohio 44127
216-271-2400
   Chief Executive and
       Franchise Director:
       James J. Mamick,
       President

**ORANGE JULIUS OF
    AMERICA**
Fast-food restaurants
3219 Wilshire Blvd.
Santa Monica, California
    90403
   Franchise Director: Keith
       Roper, Director of
       Franchise Sales

**PAINTMASTER
    AUTO/TRUCK PAINT
    CENTERS**
*Automotive repair and
    refinishing shops*
121 South Highland Mall
Pittsburgh, Pennsylvania
    15206
412-362-4440
   Franchise Director: Philip
       Borner

THE PANCAKE HOUSE,
INC.
*Restaurant owners and
franchisors*
9309 Montgomery Ave.
Cincinnati, Ohio 45242
513-984-4300
Franchise Director: Wyman
Nelson, Franchise
Agent

PARTIME/DIVISION OF
ADIA TEMPORARY
SERVICES, INC.
Employment services
Valley Forge Plaza, Suite 750
King of Prussia, Pennsylvania
19406
215-265-8700
Franchise Director: Brian
G. Dailey, Vice
President, Operations

PASQUALE FOOD
COMPANY, INC.
Pizza restaurants
19 West Oxmoor Road
Birmingham, Alabama 35209
205-942-3371
Franchise Director: Lester
Nuby, Jr., Executive
Vice President

PEDRO'S FOOD SYSTEMS, INC.
Mexican restaurants
P.O. Box 622
Columbus, Mississippi 39701
601-327-8921
Franchise Director: Louis P.
May

PENN JERSEY AUTO STORES, INC.
Automotive aftermarket merchandise
9901 Blue Grass Road
Philadelphia, Pennsylvania
19114
215-671-9901
Franchise Director: James
L. Rounds, Vice
President

PERSONNEL POOL OF AMERICA, INC.
Temporary help services
521 South Andrews Avenue
Fort Lauderdale, Florida
33301
305-764-2200
Franchise Director: Richard
L. Myers, Vice
President

PET MANAGEMENT
  SERVICES, INC.
Retail pet centers
8419 Sanford Drive
Richmond, Virginia 23228
804-266-2433
  Franchise Director: Clyde
    H. Treffeisen,
    Executive Vice
    President

PIER 1 IMPORTS, INC.
Home decor and gift items
2520 West Freeway
Fort Worth, Texas 76102
817-335-7031
  Franchise Director: Jerold
    D. Schultz, Director
    Associate Store
    Department

PIONEER TAKE OUT
  CORP.
Fast-food restaurants
3663 West Sixth Street
Los Angeles, California 90020
213-487-4820
  Franchise Director: Paul
    Wilmoth, Vice
    President, Franchise
    Sales and Public
    Relations

PIZZA DELIGHT CORP.
Fast-food restaurants
331 Elmwood Drive
Moncton, New Brunswick
Canada E1C 8T6
506-855-7795
Franchise Director: Wagdy
Galal, Vice President,
Operations

PIZZA HUT, INC.
Restaurant industry
P.O. Box 428
Wichita, Kansas 67207
316-681-9595
Franchise Director: Frank
Holdraker, Vice
President of Restaurant
Franchising

PLYWOOD MINNESOTA, INC.
*Retail home-improvement
centers*
5401 East River Road
Minneapolis, Minnesota
55421
612-560-5050
Rudy Boschwitz, President

POLY-OLEUM CORP.
Auto rustproofing
16135 Harper Avenue
Detroit, Michigan 48224
313-882-4600
William C. McKay,
President

POPEYE'S FRIED
    CHICKEN, INC.
*Fried chicken and related
    products*
800 Commerce East, Suite 310
New Orleans, Louisiana
    70123
504-733-4300
    Chief Executive: Alvin C.
        Copeland

POP SHOPPES OF
    AMERICA
Soft drink bottlers
1201 Eighteenth Street, Suite
    240
Denver, Colorado 80202
303-629-7333
    Franchise Director:
        Christopher W. Z.
        Hovey, Executive Vice
        President

POSTAL INSTANT PRESS
Instant printing
8201 Beverly Boulevard
Los Angeles, California 90048
213-653-8750
    Larry Cummings, National
        Franchise Sales
        Director

QUALITY CARE, INC.
*Hospital and home health
    care services*
65 Roosevelt Avenue
Valley Stream, New York
    11580
212-895-5992
    Franchise Director: Herman
        M. Schuster, President

QUIK STOP MARKETS,
    INC.
Convenience market chain
P.O. Box 4567 Enterprise
    Street
Fremont, California 94538
415-657-8500
    Franchise Director: Larry
        Kranich, Vice President

RADIO SHACK
Retail consumer electronics
1600 One Tandy Center
Ft. Worth, Texas 76102
817-390-3381
    Franchise Director: Robert
        R. Lynch, Vice
        President

RAMADA CAMP INNS
*Division of Ramada Inns,
    Inc.*
3838 East Van Buren
Phoenix, Arizona 85008
602-273-4460
    M. William Isbell,
        President

RAMADA INNS, INC.
Motor hotels
3838 East Van Buren
Phoenix, Arizona 85008
602-273-4000
    Franchise Director: Norman
        Thomas, Assistant Vice
        President, Franchise
        Administration

RAMPART INDUSTRIES,
    INC.
Fire and burglar alarms
One Oxford Valley, Suite 317
Langhorne, Pennsylvania
    19047
215-752-2210
    Designee: Marvin B.
        Sharfstein, President

REALTY, USA
*Real estate marketing and
    referral services*
3855 Lucas and Hunt Road
St. Louis, Missouri 63121
314-389-1111
    Thomas J. Malone,
        President

REALTY WORLD CORP.
Real estate franchisor
1001 Connecticut Avenue,
    NW
Washington, D.C. 20036
202-331-0007
    Franchise Director: Jerry
        Cole, Vice President,
        Marketing

THE RED BARN SYSTEM
Fast food
6845 Elm Street
McLean, Virginia 22101
703-893-2111
    Franchise Director: Richard
        Hohman, President

RED CARPET CORP. OF
    AMERICA
Real estate franchising
1990 North California Street,
    Suite 830
Walnut Creek, California
    94596
415-939-4550
    Anthony J. Yniguez,
        President

RON'S KRISPY FRIED
    CHICKEN
Fried chicken restaurants
6006 Bellaire Boulevard, Suite
    211
P.O. Box 250
Bellaire, Texas 77401
713-661-0811
    Franchise Director: Bob Bly

ROTH YOUNG
    PERSONNEL SERVICE,
    INC.
Middle and upper
    management employment
    services
43 West Forty-second Street
New York, New York 10036
212-869-0300
    David Roth, President

ROTO-ROOTER CORP.
Sewer and drain cleaning
services
300 Ashworth Road
West Des Moines, Iowa 50265
515-223-1343
  Franchise Director: M. B.
    McCoy

ROUND TABLE
  FRANCHISE CORP.
Pizza restaurants
1101 Embarcadero Road
Palo Alto, California 94303
415-321-4760
  Franchise Director: Steve
    Linsley, President

ROXBURY OF AMERICA,
  INC.
d.b.a. Uncle Johns'
  Restaurants
9808 Wilshire Boulevard
Beverly Hills, California
  90212
213-878-3030
  Franchise Director: Leonard
    Hill, Vice President,
    Finance

ROY ROGERS FAMILY
  RESTAURANTS
Fast-food restaurants
5161 River Road
Washington, D.C. 20016
301-986-5000
  Franchise Director: Donald
    Rodis

RUG CRAFTERS
Yarn craft stores
3321 South Fairview Street
Santa Ana, California 92704
714-540-9736
    Franchise Director: Al Hoff,
        National Franchise
        Director

SAGA ENTERPRISES, INC.
Public restaurants
One Saga Lane
Menlo Park, California 94025
415-854-5150
    James W. Morrell,
        President

SALES CONSULTANTS
INTERNATIONAL,
INC.
Sales, sales management,
    marketing, personnel
    placement
1015 Euclid Ave.
Cleveland, Ohio 44115
216-696-1122
    Franchise Director: Robert
        A. Angell, Vice
        President, Franchise
        Marketing

SANFORD ROSE
ASSOCIATES
Personnel agency
265 South Main Street
Akron, Ohio 44308
216-762-6211
    Franchise Director: George
        Mild, Vice President

SERVICEMASTER
   INDUSTRIES, INC.
*Home and office cleaning
   services*
2300 Warrenville Road
Downers Grove, Illinois 60515
312-964-1300
   Franchise Director: R. G.
      Knapp, Vice President

SERARE COURTE PAILLE
Steak house restaurants
Autoroute A6-CE 1412
Evry Cedex 91019 France
   Chief Executive: Philippe
      Hielbronner, President
      Directeur General

SERVPRO INDUSTRIES,
   INC.
*Complete on-location
   cleaning system*
11357 Pyrites Way
Rancho Cordova, California
   95670
916-635-3111
   Franchise Director: Talbert
      Denney, President

SHAKEY'S INC.
Pizza restaurants
5565 First International
   Building
Dallas, Texas 75270
800-527-7808
   Franchise Director: Larry I.
      Tate, Executive Vice
      President

SHERATON INNS, INC.
Hotels and inns, worldwide
470 Atlantic Avenue
Boston, Massachusetts 02210
617-482-1250
Franchise Director: Glen
Theirwechter, Vice
President, Director of
Franchise Development

SIR WAXER, INC.
Retail auto waxing facilities
105 West Michigan
Milwaukee, Wisconsin 53203
414-273-2200
Franchise Director: John D.
Foley, President

SMALL BUSINESS
ADVISORS, INC.
Income tax services
48 West Forty-eighth Street
New York, New York 10036
212-869-9642
Joseph Gelb, Chief Operating
Financial Officer

SONIC INDUSTRIES, INC.
Drive-in restaurants
6800 North Bryant
Route 1, Box 261
Oklahoma City, Oklahoma
73111
405-478-0731
Franchise Director: Jerry
Asher, Director of
Franchising

THE SOUTHLAND CORP.
Convenience stores
2828 North Haskell
Dallas, Texas 75230
214-828-7816
Franchise Director: Frank
Kitchen, Regional
Manager, Franchising

SPRING CREST CO.
Retail drapery stores
505 West Lambert Road
Brea, California 92621
714-529-9993
Franchise Director: Thomas
M. King, Director of
Franchising

STANLEY STEEMER
CARPET CLEANER
Carpet and furniture cleaning
4654 Kenny Road
Columbus, Ohio 43220
614-457-1733
Franchise Director: Wesley
C. Bates, Vice President

STEAMATIC, INC.
*Carpet, furniture, and drapery
cleaning*
1601 109th Street
Grand Prairie, Texas 75050
214-647-1244
Franchise Director: Lindy
Berry, Vice President
and General Manager

STEWART'S DRIVE-INS
Fast-food restaurants
1420 Crestmont Avenue
Camden, New Jersey 08103
609-966-7500
    Franchise Director: Michael
        W. Fessler, Vice
        President, Franchising

STEWART SANDWICHES
    INTERNATIONAL,
    INC.
*Manufacturer and wholesale
    distributor of frozen
    sandwiches*
5732 Curlew Drive
Norfolk, Virginia 23502
804-424-1825
    Franchise Director: W. S.
        Henderson, Director,
        Franchise Relations

THE STRAW HAT
    RESTAURANT CORP.
Pizza family restaurants
6400 Village Parkway
Dublin, California 94566
415-829-1500
    Franchise Director: John
        Shepanek, Vice
        President

STRETCH & SEW, INC.
Retail knit fabric stores
220 Seneca Street
Eugene, Oregon 97402
503-686-9961
    Franchise Director and
        Legal Counsel:
        Howard Ollis, Vice
        President

STUCKEY'S, INC.
Candies, gasoline, food
    service, gifts
P.O. Box 370
Eastman, Georgia 31023
912-374-4381
    Franchise Director: Jack
        Langhorne

SUCCESS MOTIVATION
    INSTITUTE, INC.
Motivation, education, and
    communication courses
5000 Lakewood Drive
P.O. Box 7614
Waco, Texas 76710
817-776-1230
    Paul J. Meyer, President

SVEDEN HOUSE
    INTERNATIONAL,
    INC.
Smorgasbord restaurants
1200 Multifoods Building
Minneapolis, Minnesota
    55402
612-340-3300
    Franchise Director: Kenneth
        H. Kuhn

SWENSEN'S ICE CREAM CO.
Ice cream parlors
915 Front Street
San Francisco, California 94111
415-989-8466
   Darryl A. Hart, Senior Vice
      President

SWISS COLONY STORES, INC.
Cheese and specialty food retail stores
1112 Seventh Avenue
Monroe, Wisconsin 53566
608-328-8500
   John Grey Davis, Vice
      President, Franchise
      Development

TACO BELL
Fast-food restaurants
17381 Red Hill Avenue
Irvine, California 92714
714-754-0500
   John C. O'Donnell, Vice
      President of
      Franchising

TACO TICO, INC.
Fast-food Mexican restaurant chain
3305 East Douglas
Wichita, Kansas 67218
316-686-7456
   Jim Conley, Director of
      Franchising

**TACO TIME
INTERNATIONAL,
INC.**
Drive-in fast-food restaurants
3880 West Eleventh Avenue
P.O. Box 2056
Eugene, Oregon 97402
503-687-8222
    Franchise Director: Donald
        L. Payne, Vice
        President, Marketing

TANDYCRAFTS, INC.
*Retail sale of leathercraft,
    needleart, and handicraft
    supplies*
1700 One Tandy Center
Fort Worth, Texas 76102
817-390-3015
    Franchise Director: Olsen S.
        Moses, Director, Dealer
        Division

TAYLOR RENTAL CORP.
*General purpose rental
    centers*
570 Cottage Street
Springfield, Massachusetts
    01104
413-781-7730
    Franchise Director: Wilbert
        L. Bourque, Vice
        President, Rental Sales

TEAM CENTRAL, INC.
Electronic products
720 Twenty-ninth Avenue SE
Minneapolis, Minnesota
    55414
612-331-8511
    Franchise Director: James
        H. Keefer, Vice
        President, Franchise
        Operations

TELECHECK SERVICES,
    INC.
Check verification service
1777 South Bellaire, Suite 400
Denver, Colorado 80222
303-753-9498
    Franchise Director: Robert
        J. Baer, President

TEMPACO, INC.
*Heating, air conditioning,
    refrigeration*
Drawer No. 7667
Orlando, Florida 32804
305-898-3456
    Franchise Director: David
        L. McDuffie, President

TIFFANY'S BAKERIES,
    INC.
Retail "exhibition" bakeries
40 University Avenue
Toronto, Ontario
Canada M5J 1T1
416-863-0747
    Chris Cairns, Director of
        Franchising

TUFF-KOTE DINOL, INC.
Automotive rustproofing
13650 East Ten Mile Road
P. O. Box 306
Warren, Michigan 48090
313-776-5000
  Greg Maczik, Director of
    Franchising

TUNEX, INC.
Automotive tune-up services
556 East 2100, South
Salt Lake City, Utah 84106
801-486-8133
  Delano C. Freeze,
    Chairman

UNICARE SERVICES, INC.
*Multiple service corporation-
  health care, restaurants,
  retailing, wholesaling of
  toys, and real estate
  development*
105 West Michigan Street
Milwaukee, Wisconsin 53203
414-273-2200
  Joseph J. Zilber, President

UNIFORCE SERVICES,
    INC.
Temporary personnel service
1335 Jericho Turnpike
New Hyde Park, New York
    11040
516-437-3300
  John Fanning, President

UNION PRESCRIPTION CENTERS, INC.
Prescription centers
105 West Michigan Street
Milwaukee, Wisconsin 53203
414-271-6011
   Franchise Director: George
      C. Schlinder, Franchise
      Sales Director

UNITED RENT-ALL, INC.
Equipment rentals
10131 National Boulevard
Los Angeles, California 90034
213-836-4900
   Franchise Director: Mark
      Cassell, National
      Franchise Sales
      Director

VAKUM VULK U.S., INC.
Sale of precured retread
   rubber
P.O. Box 657
Muscatine, Iowa 52761
319-262-1271
   Betty J. Lucas, Franchise
      Control Manager

VILLAGE INN PIZZA PARLORS, INC.
Pizza parlor restaurants
4221 Winfield Scott Plaza
Scottsdale, Arizona 85251
602-994-8181
   Franchise Director: F.
      Michael Carroll,
      Executive Vice
      President

WATERCARE CORP.
*Manufacturers of water
    conditioning and all
    component parts*
1520 North Twenty-fourth
    Street
Manitowoc, Wisconsin 54220
414-682-6823
    Franchise Director: William
        W. Granger, President

**WENDY'S
    INTERNATIONAL,
    INC.**
Quick-service restaurants
4288 West Dublin-Granville
    Road
P.O. Box 256
Dublin, Ohio 43017
614-889-0900
    Franchise Director: David
        Teal, Vice President,
        Franchising

**WESTERN AUTO SUPPLY
    CO.**
*Wholesale, retailer, hardware,
    home, auto items*
2107 Grand
Kansas City, Missouri 64108
816-421-6700
    Franchise Director: R. T.
        Renfro, Vice President

WAUSAU HOMES, INC.
Home manufacturing
P.O. Box 1204
Wausau, Wisconsin 54401
715-359-7272
    Earl Schuette, Chairman

WHATABURGER SYSTEMS
Fast food
3104 South Alameda
Corpus Christi, Texas 78404
512-882-2912
    Franchise Director: Thomas
        E. Dobson, Vice
        President

WHITE HEN PANTRY
    DIVISION, JEWEL
    COMPANIES, INC.
Convenience food stores
666 Industrial Drive
Elmhurst, Illinois 60126
312-833-3100
    Franchise Director: Robert
        L. Swanson

WICKS 'N' STICKS, INC.
Manufacture and sale of retail
    candles and candle
    related items
6937 Flintlock
Houston, Texas 77040
713-466-4125
    Franchise Director: Stan
        Levy, Director of
        Franchise Sales

EDWIN K. WILLIAMS &
CO.
*Bookkeeping, business
counseling, and systems
for small businesses*
5324 Ekwill Street
Santa Barbara, California
93111
805-964-4768
Franchise Director: Gene
H. Loeppke, Vice
President

WORLD BAZAAR IMPORT
STORES
Division of Munford, Inc.
P.O. Box 304
Conley, Georgia 30027
404-363-1440
James S. Cooper, Director
of Sales

WRANGLER WRANCH
FRANCHISING
SYSTEMS, INC.
*Manufacturer of wearing
apparel*
335 Church Court
Greensboro, North Carolina
27420
919-373-3400
Franchise Director: N. A.
Considine, Vice
President, Marketing

YELLOW PAGES TABEX,
    INC.
Yellow page advertising
15910 Ventura Blvd.
Encino, California 91436
213-990-6560
    James A. Davies, President

ZANTIGO MEXICAN-
    AMERICAN
    RESTAURANT
Fast food restaurants
P.O. Box 32070
Louisville, Kentucky 40232
502-459-8600
    Chief Executive: James H.
        Wille, President

ZIEBART
    INTERNATIONAL
    CORP.
Rustproofing service
P.O. Box 1290
Troy, Michigan 48099
313-588-4100
    Franchise Director: A. Ward
        Stoddard, Vice
        President

Index